Enjoy!
Dylan :)

DYLAN'S CANDY BAR
UNWRAP YOUR SWEET LIFE

DYLAN LAUREN
WITH SHERYL BERK

PHOTOGRAPHS BY QUENTIN BACON

CLARKSON POTTER
NEW YORK

Copyright © 2010 by Dylan Lauren

Published in the United States by Clarkson Potter/Publishers,
an imprint of the Crown Publishing Group, a division of
Random House, Inc., New York.
www.crownpublishing.com
www.clarksonpotter.com

CLARKSON POTTER is a trademark and POTTER with
colophon is a registered trademark of Random House, Inc.

®/™ M&M'S is a registered trademark of Mars,
Incorporated and its affiliates. This mark is used with permission.
Mars, Incorporated is not associated with Clarkson Potter/Publishers,
© Mars, Inc. 2010.

Grateful acknowledgment is made to Taradam Music, Inc., for permission to reprint lyrics from "Pure Imagination," words and music by
Leslie Bricusse and Anthony Newley, copyright © 1970–1971.

Library of Congress Cataloging-in-Publication Data
Lauren, Dylan.
   Dylan's candy bar : unwrap your sweet life / Dylan
Lauren. — 1st ed.
1. Candy.   2. Dylan's Candy Bar (Stores).   3. Lauren, Dylan.
4. Holidays in art.   I. Title.
      TX791.L32   2010
         641.8'53—dc22   2009047740

ISBN 978-0-307-45182-8

Printed in China

Design by Jennifer K. Beal Davis

Photographs by Quentin Bacon

For additional photo credits, see page 222.

10 9 8 7 6 5 4 3 2 1

First Edition

To my parents—I am the luckiest girl to have two heroes to learn from and be mentored by. You have helped make my dreams come true, and I can't thank you enough! I love you.

To the best brothers one could ever have, Andrew and David. Thank you for demonstrating such a passion for my brand and for constantly helping me to think outside the (candy) box.

To Paul—you are sweeter than candy. Thank you for being my rock. And for making me smile every day.

CONTENTS

ACKNOWLEDGMENTS

Thank you to my family, friends, and to the Dylan's Candy Bar team for their encouragement and belief in me and my brand. Special thanks to Katie—my favorite singer and crafting queen; Lauren, Rashida, and Allie for being mega-organized and helpful; Maggy for her tenacity and mother-like support; Dana and Kristin for their dedication and loyalty; Andrea for her contagious enthusiasm; Mayumi, Shar, and Dan for technical support with empathy. Thanks to Roger, Craig, Simon, Carter, and Ken for their brilliant mentoring. To Party Rental Ltd., the best one-stop shop. Thanks to Quentin, Lauren, and Michael, whose vibrant photography captured my vision. To the Clarkson Potter team: Lauren, Doris, Aliza; Emily, who made this a fun learning adventure; Marysarah, a creative genius and angel; and Jenny, who understood candy colors and graphics. To Sheryl, my superhero partner-in-writing who captured my voice and made this a blast; to the diligent Andy and Karen; and especially the NCA and all the awesome candy companies that have been so generous to me and make this industry so much fun to be a part of.

CONFESSIONS OF A CANDY GIRL

CHRONICLES OF A CANDY QUEEN

I love candy, and not just in an "I need a sugar fix" kind of sense. I love how it makes me feel. I love the sweet scents and flavors; the vibrant colors; the millions of unique shapes, sizes, and textures it comes in; the creative packaging and the eye-popping graphics. To me, candy is more than an accessible everyday product we consume; candy is an artful masterpiece!

Candy has always been an integral part of my life and who I am; if there is a chromosome for candy addict, I have it. Strangely enough, nobody else in my family shares my obsession to quite the same degree. My mom comes close, though: she always keeps a stash of dark chocolate and Peanut M&M's. My dad loves halvah, chocolate-covered pretzels, dark almond bark, and buttercrunch. My brother Andrew understands that Charleston Chews taste great frozen and Heath Bars enhance ice cream. My brother David thinks Whatchamacallits are one of the best-tasting (and best-named) candy bars, and occasionally reminisces about the Reggie Bar. But I am all about *all* candy and always have been, since I was old enough to lick my first lollipop!

I believe in candy, not just for the endorphin high it gives when consumed but also for its ability to transcend time, space, and a really bad hair day. Candy is magic! Candy is imagination! Candy is art! Candy is always in fashion! Candy is joy! Candy is memories! And candy is childhood—the best and brightest moments you wish could have lasted forever. Candy represents all the most amazing things the universe has to offer, in one irresistible package. At different points in my life, candy has been my inspiration, my motivation, even my salvation. Call me crazy, but I believe that when life sucks, there is no better remedy than to reach for an all-day sucker!

Because I see the world through candy-colored lenses and "can take tomorrow, dip it in a dream, separate the sorrow and collect up all the cream" (from the song "The Candy Man"), a lot of people refer to me as "The Candy Queen" or the "modern-day Willy Wonka." For me, these are nice compliments, but I have yet to figure out how to get a chocolate river running though the middle of America. I remember the first time I saw the movie *Willy Wonka and the Chocolate Factory*. My parents screened it at our house for my sixth birthday party. I watched in awe as the scene in Wonka's factory unfolded: the beautiful lollipop and candy cane trees, the enormous gumball statues on the pedestals, red mushrooms filled with whipped butter cream, the gigantic rainbow gummy bears dangling from colorful tree branches. Okay, the Oompa Loompas with their orange faces and green hair freaked me out a little. But beyond that, I was absolutely captivated.

My brother David and I must have watched that movie more than a hundred times through the years, and its theme song, "Pure Imagination," became my personal mantra:

There is no life I know to compare with pure imagination

Living there you'll be free if you truly wish to be . . .

Anything you want to, do it.

Wanta change the world? There's nothing to it.

I wanted to live in Wonka's world, which, in a way, I did, not solely through the candy emporiums I've created but also through the candies I associate with different eras of my life. At five, I lost my tooth eating a gooey piece of pink taffy (my brother joked that it must have been my sweet tooth, but no such luck!). In elementary school, I was hooked on cherry Swedish Fish and once bought a whole case of 300 at the corner deli. When I brought them home, my mom—fearing I'd ingest them all at once—rationed a few a day and hid the rest in her closet. It didn't take me long to find the stash, excitedly tear off the wrappers, and shove as many as I could into my mouth. However, in the process, something seemed *fishy*—they didn't taste right. I soon realized that the closet was filled with perfume sachets and, sadly, the Swedish Fish had absorbed the odor. I couldn't even find one that didn't reek of wisteria or jasmine! It was cruel and unusual punishment!

As a tween, my taste turned to red licorice—the mile-long shoelace variety, to be exact. I liked to braid it when I was bored. I lived for Candy Canteen at

camp and always went for the strawberry Twizzlers. I studied the selection, not-ing that this was one of the longer lasting items.

In high school, I was big on Bazooka and Dubble Bubble gum. I would buy several king-size tubs and chew about fifty pieces of gum in one sitting, especially to help me concentrate doing homework. I was obsessed with collect-ing all the Bazooka comics and sending away for the prizes.

It was also at this time that I stumbled on one of my biggest candy crushes: Cadbury Crème Eggs. To this day, my friends will still text me when the first ones appear in stores, a few weeks before Easter. In fact, London is one of my favorite cities, particularly because they carry Cadbury Crème Eggs almost year-round. Even the vending machines in the Tube carry them!

I remember when I was anxiously studying for my SATs and desperately needed a sugar fix. Yet one of the biggest snowstorms had hit New York. The snow was so high that streets were closed, cabs went off duty, and stores shut their doors early. The only store open was a mile away. Still, I knew that if I simply could crack into a chocolate egg and eat the creamy yellow and white fondant, I'd be able to cram all night. After all, **"stressed spelled backwards is desserts!"** So I made my mom walk in 10 feet of snow with me to the only open supermarket. I'm not sure my mom was convinced or that she appreciated trudging across the frozen tundra at midnight to get the Crème Eggs—until I proved their power by rocking the test.

When I applied for colleges, candy also played a part. The essay question asked applicants to describe themselves by comparing themselves to a food, place, or object. After writing so many entrance essays, this one was a "piece of cake"! Mine was titled "Why I Am Like an Everlasting Gobstopper." I wrote something to the effect, "A Gobstopper (jawbreaker) is well-rounded and comprised of many lay-ers. It's bright and colorful. It's strong on the outside, soft and sweet on the inside, and makes people who spend time with it very happy." I got into that college!

While I was in college studying art history and film, I got hooked on cherry gumballs. While students were collecting quarters for the laundry machine, I was

Me at eight at my brother's birthday party admiring the lollipop tree.

collecting them for the gumball machine. I'd seek out giant gumball machines at stores and supermarkets and wait persistently (often putting in a dozen quarters!) until the red gumball came down the shoot. College was also the start of my marshmallow addiction. My college roommates wanted to kill me when they'd pour out a bowl of Lucky Charms cereal, only to discover they weren't so lucky after all: I'd already extracted all the marshmallow charms. And the cafeteria staff knew me on a first-name basis because of how I liked to order my frozen yogurt: 1 cup of frozen yogurt with 3 cups of Marshmallow Fluff on top. Is there any other way to eat it?

When I graduated, I suddenly faced the typical pressure of figuring out what I should do with the rest of my life. Chewing gumballs and eating bags of mini-marshmallows were not viable occupations. But I felt in my gut that my love for candy would somehow fit into my future. I knew I wanted to do something entrepreneurial—something I was passionate about, something artistic and creative. But I couldn't pinpoint exactly what this could be. I had always admired my mother for pursuing her passions and becoming a talented photographer, author, and artist; and my dad for being an intuitive genius and visionary, and for building the greatest fashion empire and lifestyle brand. I thought of working for my dad at Polo Ralph Lauren, but I also was encouraged to start my own pursuits and make a name for myself. My parents gave me the most helpful advice: they said to do what I'm passionate about because that's when I'll be most happy and successful. They also influenced me to always follow my gut and not allow negative types or naysayers to make me doubt my dreams and ambition.

I kept this in mind as I traveled after college, throughout Europe and Asia. I loved the adventure of traveling, and I felt inspired learning about the history and culture of the world around me. I became a great explorer (of candy, that is), discovering some of the most unique candy stores around the globe. I found a candy hut in Thailand where they stocked caramelized beetles and cockroaches. In Jamaica, Rastafarians merrily pointed out their fields of sugarcane. In Italy, I found chocolatiers who must have been relatives of Michelangelo or Leonardo! They created impressive, gigantic sculptures of landmarks such as the Vatican and the Leaning Tower of Pisa out of chocolate! In Japan, geishas gave me presents of sweet bean paste and candied shrimp, delicately packaged in beautiful silk pouches. And when I took a road trip across the United States, I looked forward to late-night journeys to the massive 24-hour supermarkets to discover all the newest inventions and graphics in the candy and cereal aisles.

I returned from each trip with suitcases stuffed not with clothes or touristy souvenirs but with tons of precious confections. My house became filled with shelves of these "not to eat—just to look at" treats. To me, they were Pop Art to be admired. I was growing what is now one of the largest candy collections in the world. I was so inspired by the candy artisans I encountered, the designs of the candy and the artists I had read about in college, that I thought perhaps I'd become a Pop Artist myself and use candy as my medium. I made mosaics out of colored gumballs, M&M's, and jelly beans. I découpaged chairs and tables with gum and chocolate wrappers. I built papier-mâché sculptures and covered them with the brand mascots from candy and cereal packaging. Those illustrations of icons, like the Nesquik Rabbit and Toucan Sam, were art to me. I thought of opening a gallery/café to showcase my candy collection and artwork, as well as that of other emerging artists who worked with food. Such a space, I knew, would take time to find and create. So I continued to brainstorm while starting a boutique events firm. Even then, everything kept coming back to candy. At a winter charity event at an ice-skating rink, I decorated all the tables with white-and-silver–foiled candies and gave out coconut snowballs as favors. At a Valentine's Day benefit, I used Conversation Heart boxes as the invitations. Red Hots, Kisses, and chocolate roses were the table centerpieces.

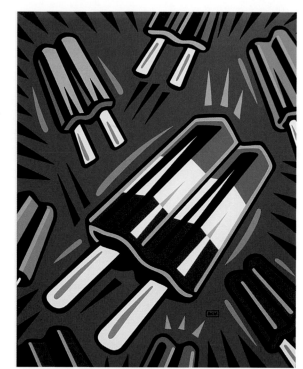

My brothers fueled my mind with clever ideas for candy products and marketing, inspiring me to take this concept further. I imagined owning a retail space that would host events and display candy and food art. I loved the thematic environments of Disney World, the mind-blowing set designs of a Janet or Michael Jackson concert, and stores like Ralph Lauren, Nike Town, Hamleys, and FAO Schwarz. They made me want to develop my own candy "retail-tainment" concept.

Then one day fate stepped in. A friend stopped me on the street to introduce his friend Jeff. He said, "You guys need to talk! You have a lot in common." Jeff was the genius behind creating FAO Schweetz (the candy store in FAO Schwarz), where I frequently shopped for inspira-

Me at age eight enjoying a milkshake.

tion. In a city of 8 million people, I met my candy soul mate right outside my doorstep! Of course, we clicked, and together we came up with a concept for a retail space that would be a mesmerizing, virtual "candy land." After a year and a half of planning, and setting up accounts with tons of candy, fancy food, and gift vendors, we were finally set to open Dylan's Candy Bar, in Manhattan, in 2001. Then September 11 happened. No one knew what the future of New York City or the world would be. New York retail was down. Tourism was at an all-time low. People were frightened, shocked, and grieving. How could anyone care about candy?

We were nervous to open, but we decided to give it a try in October. The minute we unlocked the doors to the first flagship Dylan's Candy Bar on Sixtieth Street and Third Avenue in New York City, we were flooded with customers—literally packed wall to wall. As soon as people walked in the door, their faces lit up, seeing a giant sculptural 10-foot-high chocolate bunny mascot; a humongous glass lollipop tree; candy cane columns; walls, ceilings, staircase, even chairs and tables embedded with a candy-copia of colors and sweets. As I looked around, I couldn't stop smiling. This was everything I had envisioned—and more! And I wasn't the only one who felt renewed, happy, and hopeful: New Yorkers who had lost someone in the Towers came up to me in tears, saying, "Thank you for creating such a happy haven!" Other customers, particularly those fifty years and older, would come specifically to see our collection of nostalgic candy. They liked it because it took them back to their childhood, when life was carefree and America felt strong and safe.

I was so thrilled, not just because Dylan's Candy Bar was an instant success but also because I was doing something that contributed to making people feel happy again. Eventually, Jeff and I decided to go in different directions, but we remain candy soul mates. Since 2001, I have opened several Dylan's Candy Bar locations across the United States, with many more plans on the horizon.

I knew I'd arrived when two of my biggest idols—Martha Stewart and Oprah Winfrey—invited me on their TV shows to share my expertise about candy. When Oprah announced Dylan's Candy Bar was "quickly becoming an American icon" and a "must-see destination," I thought I had gone to candy heaven! However, even with that kind of endorsement, I knew I couldn't just rest on my Reese's Peanut Butter Cups. Because what I have learned, I want to share. I think it's the true message, the "bigger picture," so to speak, of why I went into the candy business.

I believe you can live "the sweet life" every day, not just on holidays or special occasions, or when that time-of-the-month craving strikes. Candy is for everyday and everybody—no matter what age, gender, or cultural background. Take a minute and think back to your favorite candy memory. How do you feel? Elated? Excited? Invincible? What if you could feel that way all the time? As you turn the pages, you will unwrap mouthwatering photos of gorgeous candies, candy fun facts, and quizzes. There are helpful tips on how new and classic candies can be assembled in a totally innovative light, so tabletops, decorations, and gifts become incredibly memorable and stylish. But look a little deeper. Keep licking that Blow Pop till you reach the bubble-gum center!

What's hidden in here is every way candy can inspire you, uplift you, and transform the ordinary into the extraordinary.

I hope this book will help awaken your creative spirit and inner child and make you feel, every day, "like a kid in a candy store."

CANDY QUIZ

ARE YOU A TRUE CANDY GIRL OR BOY?

If you answer *yes* to five or more of the following, you're a lady or gent who loves sweets (welcome to the club!):

❏ I know that wearing Lucky Charms, Candy Necklaces, and Ring Pops is always in style.

❏ I would rather tie my shoes with licorice laces.

❏ Whether my friends are Smarties or Airheads, I love them equally.

❏ I know how to dance the Laffy Taffy, Tootsie Roll, and Charleston Chew.

❏ I'm addicted to Big League Chew, chocolate cigars, and Candy Cigarettes—not tobacco.

❏ I always have starlight mint breath.

❏ If needed, I'd prefer a Conversation Heart transplant.

❏ When I grow old, I'd like to walk with a candy cane.

❏ I prefer Wax Lips to Botox.

CANDY DI

If you want to whisper sweet nothings into someone's ear (or just sound cool), work these words and phrases into your conversations.

Arm candy (n.): A person of either gender whom you take to accompany you to an event because he or she is very attractive (even better than a designer purse!).

Eye candy (n.): A person or object that is beautiful (and fun to look at).

Brain candy (n.): Fun facts, trivia, and interesting tidbits of info that "feed" one's intelligence.

Daily candy (n.): News each day that's filled with fun information, trends, and the scoop on what's going (also a great website!).

Like taking candy from a baby (phrase): Extremely easy.

Sweet! (adj.): An exclamation used to express awesomeness.

Sugar coat (v.): To present information in a way that makes it seem less serious or bad.

Serve up a lollipop (v.): To make something easy for someone; to throw a batter an easy pitch to hit.

A spoonful of sugar helps the medicine go down (phrase): From the movie *Mary Poppins,* find some "fun" in any job that must be done and the job is easier to do. To mix in some good news with the bad news; to soften a painful message.

CTIONARY

Sweeten the pot (v.): To add more money, reward, bonus, or compensation; to make something more valuable.

Cop it sweet (v.): To accept the circumstances, whatever they may be.

Sweetheart deal (n.): A profitable deal or venture.

Like a kid in a candy store (adj.): Reacting with childlike enthusiasm to a situation or place.

Sugar daddy (n.): Usually an older male who is dating a younger female and spoils her with gifts and money, like a daddy might do for his daughter.

Sweetness and light (n.): Friendliness and ease.

Swimming in molasses (v.): Moving very slowly, as if you were swimming in a thick goo.

Sweet 16 and never been kissed (phrase): Innocent and naive when it comes to matters of the heart.

Cookie cutter (adj.): Ordinary; just like everything else, with no originality.

Sucker (n.): A person who's easy to fool and take advantage of.

High school sweethearts (n.): A couple who met at a young age and remain together.

Sappy (adj.): Corny or clichéd.

EYE CANDY

CANDY KALEIDOSCOPE

Sometimes candy is so beautiful, I don't even want to eat it. It pains me to pop a perfect rainbow nonpareil in my mouth, when I can sit back and admire its artistry. For this reason, I display hundreds of candies around my home, on shelves, on the coffee table, as the dining table centerpiece. I love to surround myself with their myriad colors; they keep me happy and invigorated.

To me, candy is not just something you enjoy in your mouth; it's something you savor visually as well. It's as much art to me as a Warhol or a Lichtenstein. I think I inherited my appreciation for color and art from my family. Most generations of my family are artists in some form, whether they are painters, designers, filmmakers, or dancers. We all tend to be sensitive to color and how it moves us; we express ourselves by wearing it or by decorating our personal spaces with it.

Throughout my childhood, I went into my dad's offices and watched him design clothing. I was fascinated by the brightly colored swatches of fabric in giant glass apothecary jars. I literally wanted to climb the shelves, reach into the jars, and eat the fabric! The colors were mouthwatering! This was a true case of synesthesia. I was inspired by seeing how the fall and spring collections were differentiated by shades and gradations of color: tans, olives, hunter green, and maroon for fall; and fuchsia, turquoise, and bright orange for spring. I am always drawn to the summer collection of polos and sweaters that are merchandised in a rainbow. It's challenging to pick a favorite, since each one looks even better in the midst of the other colors.

Similar to fashion, different colors of candy are emphasized during different seasons. Pastels in pink, blue, purple, green, orange, and yellow are extremely popular for spring. Bold red, emerald green, white, blue, gold, and silver are more pronounced in the winter months. But unlike fashion, it's okay to buy a candy in *any* color, even if it's not in season!

When I was designing Dylan's Candy Bar, I chose white as the backdrop. I wanted the candy colors to really leap off the shelves and out of the bins, like art displayed on a white gallery wall. The candy fixtures and architecture were created to match the colors of actual candy, so customers could feel they were in a modern Candy Land. Colors emit energy and cheer people up. The kaleidoscope of colors at Dylan's Candy Bar is one of the reasons people say it is one of "the happiest places on earth." I'm extremely particular about the colors we use when designing Dylan's Candy Bar products. I'm obsessed with the Pantone book (the color guide and my bible), and I use it to ensure everything is printed to match the candy colors. I'm a stickler; I will insist we redo items several times until they match. It will bother me all day if I feel the color is off.

When I chose the nine colors to use in my logo, my financial advisers almost had a heart attack! Most logos are one color because it's easier to print and way less expensive. But to me, the variety of color was so reminiscent of candy and so important to make our products shine apart from other brands as more unique and giftable. I learned from my dad and other successful company founders that color is crucial for brand recognition and memory. Everyone knows Tiffany blue, Barbie hot pink, and McDonald's red and yellow!

Color plays one of the biggest roles in influencing customers to buy products, from cars to shoes to candy. According to the Institute for Color Research, "people make a subconscious judgment about a person, environment or product within 90 seconds of initial viewing and 62–90% of this assessment is based on color alone." Colors also have been proven to catch shoppers' eyes and extend the time they spend looking at something.

When my team of buyers and I attend the Candy Expos, color plays a major role in deciding what products make the cut. Typically a collection that has all the rainbow colors will be bought. Our goal is for Dylan's Candy Bar to have the absolute largest variety of flavors and colors in all candy categories, from rock candy to gummy bears, from filled chocolates and gumballs to jelly beans. Color has the ability to affect mood and bring back memories. I think my customers get nostalgic for their youth when they come in the store. They see all the primary-colored candies, and they subconsciously remind them of their earlier toys and games. Suddenly their memory of first-grade art class and learning ROYGBIV (the rainbow) is evoked.

Color also has a strong impact on how people perceive products to taste or smell. We form these color-flavor associations at an early age. For example, yellow candy is typically expected to taste like fresh lemons. Customers feel rewarded when they can predict that flavor before they bite into a yellow candy.

Yet candy can also be full of surprises, and that's part of what makes it one of the most fun commodities. For example, a yellow gummy bear may unexpectedly taste like pineapple or banana; a yellow jelly bean can be flavored like popcorn! The process of discovering these unpredictable flavors becomes an adventure that brings out the inner child in anyone willing to taste.

HUE TALKING TO ME?

YELLOW is one of the three bestselling colors of candy. Perhaps that's because it's the color of the sun, and its brightness elicits a cheerful reaction. In fact, seeing yellow triggers your brain to release serotonin. And even better, it can speed up your metabolism; therefore, you can eat more candy if you surround yourself in yellow! So decorate your home with yellow candies like bowls of Lemonheads and yellow Peeps. You'll always feel optimistic and creative in its presence.

ORANGE is considered one of the most daring and exciting colors, synonymous with Halloween, Thanksgiving, and fruits like oranges, nectarines, and peaches. Since it's perceived to be warming and energizing, people expect to eat orange sweets and get a rush of energy and a dose of vitamin C.

RED is the most popular color of candy sold at Dylan's Candy Bar. Items such as red Swedish Fish, sour watermelon rinds, strawberry licorice, and cherry lollipops are among our bestsellers. Red is a common color in natural foods and is associated with fresh, juicy, flavorful foods like refreshing watermelon and even a juicy steak. Red candies usually taste like cherry, raspberry, strawberry, cranberry, watermelon, or cinnamon. It is the first color the eye notices and is drawn to. Red also uplifts and excites people, keeping customers high with energy when they shop. So, is it any wonder that sales of red candy increase during Valentine's Day and Christmas, when red is the holiday theme color associated with love and Santa's ho-ho-ho uniform?

PINK is a subtler shade of red, and like red it's associated with romance. But contrary to red, it is the most calming of the colors. Since it's symbolic of femininity, candies typically are produced in pink for baby showers or for women's causes, such as breast cancer awareness. Pink has such a variety of flavors related to it: strawberry, pink lemonade, pink grapefruit, bubble gum, and cotton candy. There is something very "kiddy" about pink: little girls love it, and it projects a princess or Barbie girl.

BLUE is another calming color. Blue candies are good to use for decorating picture frames or storage boxes because they help give a room a sense of tranquillity—like the blue of the sky or the ocean. Blue (or turquoise Pantone 3135, to be exact!) is my favorite color, and therefore I have chosen it to be the signature color of my brand. Luckily, blue is also statistically Americans' favorite color. However, it's not so popular in candy or food. Very few candies are blue. Mars was rather daring to make one of their M&M's colors blue. Blue is typically an appetite suppressant, because most natural foods in the world are not blue; we therefore think a blue food is unnatural or toxic. But it's for these same reasons that kids are most attracted to blue candies, like blue lollipops and gum that turns your tongue blue. Blue has an "alien" connotation: the grosser the better!

GREEN is the color of things found growing in nature, like grass, trees, and fresh vegetables. Since environmental concerns have become very topical, most products that are now organic or packaged in recycled materials are green. Green is also a popular candy color for health enthusiasts. Green candy is usually flavored with lime, apple, kiwi, pear, or spearmint. And when fashion trends dictate lime green as "in," fashion victims will probably purchase green candies, such as lime fruit slices and apple fruit rings.

PURPLE is a popular color used by companies trying to appeal to young girls, as studies show it's the most favorite color among them. Tweens love purple rock candy and Grapeheads. If you are doing a craft or cooking with candy, it's actually beneficial to use this color. It's known to stimulate brain activity and problem solving. The more nutritionally conscious seek purple candies because these are thought to include extracts of grape, pomegranate, and açaí berry. Mature and sophisticated consumers tend to appreciate purple-wrapped candies and boxes of chocolate, as purple is the most regal color and has a long history of associations with wealth, prosperity, and kings and queens.

BROWN is the color of the earth. It's a color associated with reliability, stability, and "groundedness," a smart choice for brands that want traditional, loyal consumers. It is also, of course, the color of chocolate and fudge—so there is always a rich sweetness associated with anything in this shade. Brown is also a popular color for nostalgic treats, like cola and root-beer–flavored sucking candies.

BLACK is commonly the color of licorice, dark chocolate, and pepper-infused exotic candies. It is popular at Halloween since it's synonymous with the grave, death, and evil. But it's not typically appetizing. Still, chocolate companies use black in packaging, as it's traditionally a color that represents power and shows authority in a (candy) category.

According to color studies, candy that's colorless, such as **GRAY** or **WHITE** confections, is assumed to be less potent or even lack smell and flavor. The lighter the shade of color, the creamier and softer it's expected to be, such as vanilla fudge, coconut bonbons, or marshmallows. White candies are popular for decorating a bridal shower or wedding dessert table, since white represents cleanliness and purity.

Companies often save **GOLD** for candies they claim are top of the line or have award-winning flavor. Gold or foiled candies are also prevalent for the holidays, such as foiled chocolate bells and gold-dusted chocolates. **SILVER** is used to convey that a product is reliable and sterling in quality. It shimmers like a diamond, so it's often used at weddings in the form of Hershey's Kisses, Jordan almonds, and silver-foiled sucking candies.

PURE EYE CANDY
LOLLIPOPS AND GUM

Two families of candy that are among my favorites to collect—and simply stare at—are lollipops and gum. The swirls and stripes and different shapes that lollipops come in make them art to me. And gum—particularly gumballs—come in all of the shades of color I love. I prop my office with gumball machines because looking at them makes me happy.

BRAIN CANDY
THE LOLLIPOP

Cavemen were actually the first lollipop lovers. They collected honey from beehives with sticks—and couldn't resist licking some of the sweet stuff that clung to their sticks. The name "lollipop" was created by candy maker George Smith, who owned the Bradley Smith Company. Smith thought the name of his favorite racehorse, Lolly Pop, would make a great name for the treat, and he trademarked it in 1931.

BRAIN CANDY
GUM

Gum also can be traced back to prehistoric times, when the cavemen had fun chewing on tree resin. In 200 BC, Mayans chomped chicle sap from evergreen trees. In 1848, businessman John Curtis produced and sold gum, offering two "chaws" for a penny.

Gum got a bit tastier in 1880: that's when William White decided to mix sugar and corn syrup with chicle (sweet!) and add just a touch of peppermint extract. But we have Thomas Adams Sr. to thank for gum as we know it today. He was introduced to chicle by Mexican general Antonio López de Santa Anna. Adams thought the elastic ingredient would be perfect for creating more cost-efficient car tires. He was wrong about that—but salvaged his invention! Using the chicle, he created the first manufactured gum, Black Jack.

Frank Fleer was the first to create bubble gum (which he called Blibber-Blubber). It took more than twenty years to perfect, and in 1928, it was finally ready and renamed Dubble Bubble by Walter Diemer. Most people think bubble gum is intentionally pink—after all, it is a fun color! But the truth is it was the only coloring the inventor had left, so he used it!

DYLAN'S CANDY BAR

HERETHEYARE...
PROJECT RUNWAY
Season 4
Eye Candy
Fashions
Proudly loaned to
wrappedhersheys.com

HOW TO LIVE THE SWEET LIFE . . .
WHEN EVERYTHING (AND I MEAN *EVERYTHING*)
IN YOUR WARDROBE IS BLACK

True, black is sexy and oh-so-slenderizing. But *everything* dark and dreary? Accessorize with a colorful bag filled with candy, or liven up your look with some candy-colored accessories:

- Pile on a stack of bangles in jelly bean shades: red, yellow, blue, green, and purple.

- Wear long, dangling earrings made of turquoise (think the color of blue raspberry Jolly Ranchers) to bring out your eyes and draw focus up and away from figure flaws.

- Drape a bubblegum pink pashmina over your shoulders to instantly make a little black dress look more exciting.

- Wrap a grosgrain belt with lollipop-like stripes of yellow, red, blue, and orange around your waist for a sunny, slenderizing accent.

- Carry a clutch in a lollipop shade; nothing adds regal sophistication to an outfit like a burst of grape purple!

- A rainbow-colored scarf can be a "Life Saver": tie it around your neck, on the handle of a tote, or even lace it through your belt loops.

- Wear sexy patent leather heels in Swedish Fish red to draw attention to shapely legs.

- Polish your nails in candy hues like Red Hot, cotton candy, or even lemon drop.

- Candy stripers can be sexy: add red and white striped ribbon to your hair.

BABY SHOWERS

FINDING YOUR INNER CHILD

Think back to that first allowance your parents gave you as a child—that fifty cents or (if you were really well-behaved that week) those few dollar bills. What did you spend it on? Odds are it wasn't what you splurge on today (the newest cell phone, a sexy pair of stilettos, a weekend in Las Vegas). It was probably something sticky, sweet, and packaged to perfection in a brightly colored wrapper. And nothing was as wonderful and satisfying. Life was good!

As we grow up, we are bombarded with tons of material stuff. Junk that clutters our closets, our homes, our cars, our desks, our heads! We forget that the sweetest reward is often the simplest. Kids know that. They're the lucky ones.

Children never contemplate how many grams of fat reside in a bite of chocolate. They're fearless. They'll eat the entire box of Sno-Caps without a care in the world. And they get away with things because they're too young to "know better"—like blowing their bubble gum in people's faces. They'll chomp on a Jawbreaker without fear of losing a filling (after all, they don't have to pay the dentist bill!). If chocolate gets all over their faces and hands, they don't think twice about a stain settling into their clothes (or your furniture). And if a piece of candy falls on the floor, they certainly don't think about the millions of dirty shoes that have stood on that spot. Germs or not, they won't miss a single lick or bite!

Wouldn't it be wonderful to stay a kid forever? To just live in the moment, every moment? To not think about work or worries or calories or cavities? Well, eating candy can help you do that. If you're depressed, bored, frustrated, or frazzled, I swear it is the savior and the antidote to what ails you. For me, candy provides a magical escape back to my past, back to a simpler time when life was all sweet and stress-free. I'm not saying eating confections is going to fix all your problems overnight. But it will put you in a much better mood, making you see clearly that things aren't so bad, so hopeless, so hellish.

Despite what some may think, eating candy is actually a very grown-up way of coping because it acknowledges one monumental truth: "You are what you eat." And if it's a gooey spoonful of Marshmallow Fluff or a handful of Jujyfruits, how could you be anything but really sweet and happy? Ask any kid. A candy a day (or two or three . . .) keeps the blues away.

ENTERTAINING WITH CANDY
BABY GIFTS, FAVORS, AND DECOR

Candy comes in the perfect baby-themed hues: gorgeous blues and pinks and a mixture of pastels (if the baby's gender is unknown). These colorful candies can decorate the newborn's room, cover the baby shower gift or dining table, serve as an announcement, or even better, be eaten by the proud new parents!

- Pastel Jordan almonds, licorice pastilles, jelly beans, or Satellite Wafers are good for filling baby bottles.

- Baby feet–shaped lollipops can be assembled into a creative centerpiece. The uniquely shaped lollipop favor is fun to receive.

- Candies and chocolates shaped like candy blocks, rocking horses, and rubber duckies cleverly work as decorations for the shower table atop napkins or in bowls at each setting.

- Stogies are unhealthy! The men in the family will enjoy the newborn's arrival even more with a chocolate cigar in hand.

- M&M's and Hershey's plush characters, oversized Pez dispensers, Jelly Belly clocks, Peeps pillows, Nerds, and gummy bear stationery are perfect for decorating the nursery!

- Candy-colored and -themed bedding and wallpaper can be chosen, then babies can see and feel the happy vibes from bright colors.

BRAIN CANDY
A CANDY FAMILY TREE

- The Sugar Daddy was originally called The Papa. This caramel pop was invented by a chemist in 1925 and was actually the biggest lollipop around then.

- The Sugar Mama is a chocolate-covered Sugar Daddy pop. Sadly, she was discontinued in the 1980s.

- Sugar Babies were a 1935 spin-off of the Sugar Daddy. They are mini candy-coated milk caramels. In the 1930s, "Sugar Babies" was a term used for young women on whom middle-aged "Sugar Daddies" spent lots of money.

- Sour Patch Kids were released in the United States in 1985. They were originally called Mars Men because the product's inspiration and design came in the 1970s, when many people were convinced they had seen UFOs.

CANDY ICON
THE DUCK

This cute, quacking creature is often a favorite theme for a baby shower. Why? First, there's the bath connection: this is a "shower" after all, and ducks float in bathtubs. People also associate them with a baby's toys. Then there's the Sesame Street connection: the unforgettable Ernie warbling "Rubber Duckie, You're the One." The origin of the rubber duck is not known, but the first one supposedly appeared in the 1800s, when rubber was first manufactured. Sadly, it lacked a squeaker! Note: This duckie is solid chocolate!

CANDY CRAFT
BASSINET GIFT BASKET

Step 1. Cut the Styrofoam to fit inside the bassinet.

Step 2. Cut ribbon into 6-inch pieces. Tie a bow around each lollipop stem.

Step 3. Stick lollipops facing out in two rows, so all lollipops can be seen.

Step 4. Cover remaining space with ribbon candy.

Step 5. Wrap the bassinet in cellophane and tie it with a bow.

MATERIALS

- Floral Styrofoam
- White bassinet
- 1 yard satin ribbon, in pink or blue or white
- 5 large pink or blue lollipops
- 2 pounds pink or blue ribbon candy
- Cellophane

Note: Chocolate baby shoe—too meltable to wear!

SWEET PREGNANCY REMEDIES

Many women suffer from morning sickness when they're expecting. Luckily, there are several candy ways to soothe symptoms (and since you're eating for two now, you can happily indulge!). Preggie Pops are super sour, which for many women wipes away that queasy feeling. You can also try Lemonheads, Cherry Sours, Sour Patch Kids, Wonka Sour Puckerooms, or Tear Jerkers. Ginger candies and peppermint have also been proved to relieve nausea in some women; always keep a stash of Starlight Mints in your purse!

BABY SHOWER GAMES

The most popular baby shower game at Dylan's Candy Bar is our **"DIRTY DIAPER GAME."** Unfortunately, some of the guests who play it have second thoughts about having children . . . but only for a second! Here's how: First, microwave ten different candy bars for 30 seconds each. Then scoop each melted bar into a diaper. Guests have to pick a diaper and lick the chocolate off it and guess which type of candy it is. If they guess correctly, they get a prize, such as a supply of that candy bar. If they guess wrong, they suffer the humiliation of having to lick another diaper until they guess right!

Another fun game is what I like to call **"BEDTIME STORY."** Divide the guests into teams and hand each team a list of candy names. The challenge is to write a clever bedtime story (it's even better if it's about pregnancy or parenthood) for the mom-to-be using at least ten of the names. Get as creative, silly, or sassy as you like! Have each team captain read the finished tale to the crowd. Then take a vote and award the team with the best story a prize (candy for everyone on the team!).

EXAMPLE: (You can distribute this list or read it to the teams so they get the idea.) Henry and Jill went away to the Poconos for a **RED HOT** weekend of **HUGS & KISSES.** A month later, Jill shared some wonderful news with her husband. **"O HENRY!"** she cried. "We're having a baby!" **"SKOR!"** said Henry. The couple found out they were having twin boys. "Let's name them **MIKE & IKE,**" suggested Jill. But when she got to the hospital, the **AIRHEAD** doctor revealed he'd made a little mistake: "It's not two babies . . . it's **'THREE MUSKETEERS!'"** he said. Then he handed them his bill for **100 GRAND.**

"Triplets are **GOOD & PLENTY** for us!" said Henry, mopping his brow. "It's **NUTRAGEOUS**!" cried Jill. "I'm going to be **BONKERS**!" Luckily, they hired Super Nanny—a real **LIFE SAVER**—to help them handle their newborn trio! And this gave Jill a little time off to go to the gym and tone up her postbaby **JELLY BELLY.** The End!

TOY STORY
CANDY LAND AND BARBIE

Two toy icons—Candy Land and Barbie—now have an even sweeter meaning for me. In 2009, the year of Candy Land's sixtieth anniversary, Dylan's Candy Bar became the first retailer to have its own special-edition, fully personalized Candy Land board game. Since Candy Land was one of my inspirations, this was personally a very special honor and one of the products I'm most proud of. Our customized board game allows adults to take a trip down memory lane with their families—travel through a world of sweet adventure via the Dylan's Candy Bar Unicorn Pop Forest, the Candy Button Factory, and the Candy Carnival and visit some sweet friends such as the Cotton Candy Queen and Professor Lollipop. The characters and destinations on the board will, I hope, elicit the fun of visiting Dylan's Candy Bar stores.

Candy Land actually has a fascinating history. The game was invented in the 1940s by a California woman, Eleanor Abbott, who was recovering from polio. Eleanor wanted to do something "sweet" for children afflicted with polio, something that would entertain them and make them feel better. So she approached Milton Bradley with her idea for a board game. The first Candy Land games were sold for only $1, and the ads for the game promise to fulfill "the sweet tooth yearning of the younger set without the tummyache aftereffects." It's now often the first board game a young child learns to play because it requires no reading or counting.

BARBIE
THE ULTIMATE FASHION ICON

In 2009, Barbie enjoyed the sweet life while celebrating her fiftieth anniversary with Dylan's Candy Bar! We infused sassy with sweet by blending Barbie glam-gal images and tongue-in-cheek sayings to create fun treats. Some of our bestsellers were the five-pack of chocolate bars wrapped with popular images of Barbie through five decades in fashion; a miniature shoebox with Barbie's chocolate high heels; "still in mint condition" mint tins; and pink malt balls in martini glasses that were etched "Ken can satisfy only so many cravings." Barbie collectors young and old, boy and girl, remarked, "Glamour has never tasted so good." The Dylan's Candy Bar Barbie Doll (right) launches in 2010, and that is going to be sweet!

BRAIN CANDY
CANDY LAND WHO'S WHO

Though the characters have changed a few times since the original game—and undergone several special editions—these are the Candy Land folks I love the most!

THE GINGERBREAD PEOPLE: The original playing pieces to move around the board.

THE KIDS: Lucky children who get to explore the magical world of Candy Land.

MR. MINT: He lives in Peppermint Forest and wears red and white stripes—so he looks like a tall, skinny candy cane.

GRAMMA NUTT: Nurturing but also a little nutty, she lives in Peanut Acres.

KING KANDY: The lost king and the "father" of Candy Land.

JOLLY: A cute gummy creature who lives in Gumdrop Pass.

LOLLY: A little girl with a lollipop-designed dress.

LORD LICORICE: The villain of Candy Land, Lord Licorice tries to turn everything to licorice.

PRINCESS FROSTINE: A beautiful and graceful princess who twirls around the ice in an evening gown.

GLOPPY THE MOLASSES MONSTER: A friendly monster who in later editions becomes a chocolate monster.

BIRTHDAYS

FOREVER YOUNG

When I was a kid I always looked forward to my birthday. I'd count down the days until the event. But as I've grown up, I've become increasingly depressed at the thought of my birthday's nearing. The years seem to pass faster and faster. I much prefer to acknowledge my friends' and family's birthdays than my own. I also believe the most appreciated birthday gift is to throw a little party for someone else. This way, the birthday boy or girl doesn't have to worry about all the details—or *aging*!

Candy, of course, is the perfect theme for any age because it evokes the kid in all of us! One of the things I enjoy most about my stores' party rooms is watching how much fun people, whether they're two or sixty-two, have at parties when they interact with candy. For starters, you can create candy-themed centerpieces, favors, and invitations. These are much more memorable ways to share the details with guests. Tie a card with the party specifics to a large lollipop; create stickers to place onto cello bags filled with the birthday person's favorite candy; spell out the birthday boy's name in Jujubes glued onto the cover of the invite; or customize the wrapper on a chocolate bar with the party details and birthday girl's picture.

THEME PARTY

No matter what the birthday boy or girl's sweet tooth, here are some great ideas for throwing a candy-themed birthday bash.

FOR THE CHOCOLATE LOVER

INVITATION: Customized wrappers of chocolate bars with a photo of the party person (a young or silly photo gets the most RSVPs).

GAME: Guess that Candy Bar. Guests are blindfolded and presented with ten miniature squares of various candy bars. They are given 3 minutes to taste each one and write down what the candy bar is.

ACTIVITY: Decorating Chocolate Sculptures. Guests are given a plate with the party person's themed chocolate sculpture and a "paint" palette filled with a variety of colored frostings (vanilla frosting mixed with food coloring) plus five watercolor brushes and several miniature candies (sprinkles, mini M&M's,

multicolored chocolate-covered sunflower seeds, etc.). These sculptures are also great party favors for guests to take home and eat.

BEVERAGE: Chocolate milkshakes and malteds, chocolate egg cream, hot chocolate, frozen hot chocolate.

FOOD: Chocolate Waterfall: Guests can enjoy dipping a variety of bite-size snacks, from cakes to doughnuts to pretzels, into an overflowing chocolate fountain. If white chocolate is used, it can be colored with food coloring to match the party person's favorite color.

FOR SOMEONE WITH A COLORFUL PERSONALITY
(WHO ALSO IS AN AVID GUM CHEWER)

FAVORS: Fill cellophane bags with multicolored miniature gumballs (or any colorful candy). Add a primary-colored bow and hang a tag with the guest's name to personalize it.

CENTERPIECE: A classic red gumball machine makes for a beautiful and nostalgic central piece. Tie multicolored balloons to it and the machine also functions as a paperweight. Guests can put coins in the machine and eat the gumballs during the party, and the party person will end up with the machine and some spare change to buy him- or herself a token birthday gift!

NAPKIN RINGS/DECOR: Candy Buttons are great because they have a gorgeous pattern and are like Pop Art. They are also nostalgic and therefore great for bringing out the kid in all of us, especially at a birthday party. Roll paper into a cuff around a brightly colored napkin to hold the folded napkin in place. Or bend the Candy Button paper and scatter it around the table like confetti.

GAME: Bubble Gum Blowing Contest. Who can blow the largest bubble before it bursts?

ACTIVITY: Decorate a Gumball Machine: Decorate your own 1-foot-high wooden gumball machine (sold at craft stores) using colorful markers and edible delights. Then fill it with gumballs and voilà!

or

Decorate a Picture Frame: Guests are given a 5 x 7-inch picture frame and a paint palette of colorful candies, from gumballs to gummy bears and jelly beans (wrapped or unwrapped is fine). They can decorate the border and then fill the frame with a photo from the party as a memento.

FOOD: A candy-covered birthday cake! I suggest some of the more colorful candies like Unicorn Pops, Whirly Pops, nonpareils, and candy sticks.

DRINK: Colorful Sodas: Seltzer with food coloring and colorful straws.

BIRTHDAY BLING . . .
TO MAKE YOUR MOUTH ZING!

You can also theme goody bags with candy to match the birthday person's birthstone. Birthstones are gemstones associated with the month of birth. Often they are thought to have qualities that represent the nature of the person born in that month. However, these precious stones are often expensive, and candy can look just as beautiful as gems.

- **JANUARY/GARNET:** Australian red licorice, Red Hot Dollars, Atomic Fireballs

- **FEBRUARY/AMETHYST:** Grapeheads, grape gummy bears, island punch Jelly Belly

- **MARCH/AQUAMARINE:** Cotton-candy–flavored rock candy, light blue chocolate sunflower seeds, light blue M&M's

- **APRIL/DIAMOND:** Clear rock candy, pineapple gummy bears, grapefruit sections

- **MAY/EMERALD:** Green chocolate sunflower seeds, gummy spearmint leaves, green apple licorice

- **JUNE/PEARL:** White chocolate, white Jordan almonds

- **JULY/RUBY:** Swedish Fish, Boston Baked Beans, strawberry licorice wheels

- **AUGUST/PERIDOT:** Lime green Sixlets, Sour Patch Apples, gummy Key lime berries

- **SEPTEMBER/SAPPHIRE:** Blueberry Jelly Belly, blue raspberry gummy bears, blue raspberry Sour Belts

- **OCTOBER/OPAL:** Yogurt– or white-chocolate–covered pretzels, French vanilla Jelly Belly

- **NOVEMBER/TOPAZ:** Butterscotch candy, orange gummy bears, Circus Peanuts

- **DECEMBER/TURQUOISE:** Teal M&M's, berry blue Jelly Belly, blueberry Sour Bottles

THE GIFT OF GIVING SWEETS

I believe that any day can be turned into a holiday because any day with good news is a reason to celebrate. For instance, a friend who complained nonstop finally quit the job she hated. Celebrate! Your ex is moving out of the country. Celebrate! You found an extra $20 in your pocket. Celebrate! The new season of your favorite TV show is starting. Celebrate!

And when the day isn't going your way, a little holiday mentality can really turn it around. A simple gift to yourself or to a friend to commemorate (or commiserate) is in order. Candy is that perfect present—not too pricey, not too showy (unless you want it to be). You can be as creative, crafty, or clever as you like with candy.

Sometimes a candy gift can also say what's in your heart when the words are too painful, too scary, or too difficult to speak out loud. While my aunt Susan was in the hospital for cancer, she received many gifts (everyone loved her!). My cousin gave her several colored crystal bracelets that had been blessed by healers in Brazil. My uncle gave her gorgeous new and antique bangles. She and my mom exchanged silver friendship bracelets. I brought her comfy candy pajamas and a jewelry gift—it wasn't quite as sophisticated as the other jewelry, but it definitely stood out. I gave her our Gumball Bracelet, a rainbow of glossy round beads. I wasn't sure she'd ever wear it, among all her fancy baubles, but I knew it would make her happy to see something that was bright and cheery when she was sick. To my surprise, the minute she received it, she put it on and never took it off. She said it made her smile because it was so colorful and reminded her of two things she loved: me and sweets.

A candy gift can do that. In good times and in bad, it has the power to lift the spirit and warm the heart. But what I love most is that it can create a lasting memory when you share it with someone special.

DECORATING WITH CANDY

HOMEMADE GIFTS

- Glue candy onto a picture frame. It's a fun way to display a special memory.

- Make a sweeter storage system. Cover a shoe box or an oatmeal container in candy wrappers. Display the boxes proudly on your dresser or tabletops.

- Color coordinate your rooms. Have candy dishes filled with candies that match the color of your paint.

- Instead of flowers that wilt, stick several large lollipops or sugar roses into a vase of blue jelly beans or layers of foiled candies.

- For a holiday, layer its color-themed candy in a vase and stick the flower of the season in it (pink and white Good & Plenty with a rose for Valentine's Day, red and green Jujubes and a poinsettia for Christmas, etc.).

- Make your child's lunchbox stand out at school among the trendy licensed brands—glue M&M's, Sixlets, or other hard-shelled candies onto it, then shellac to make it last the school year.

CANDY GAMES

Get your game on. At Dylan's Candy Bar, even eighty-year-olds celebrating their birthdays still find candy-related activities at their party more fun than small talk. Stage a licorice relay: Give each player a licorice lace, about a yard long. Contestants start with about an inch of licorice in their mouths, and keep their hands behind their backs at all times. On "Go," they race to finish the entire piece without ever using their hands. You can also have guests participate in licorice limbo! Instead of a pole, guests duck under a long vine of red licorice. Or take part in a timeless tradition. Invite everyone to take a whack at a candy piñata!

BRAIN CANDY
THE PIÑATA

Who knew? The origin of the piñata is actually Chinese, not Hispanic. Marco Polo discovered the Chinese making figures of cows, oxen, and buffalo, which they covered with colored paper. On the New Year, they would take a swing at the figures—but it was colorful sticks and seeds, not sweet treats, that came pouring out when the figure burst open. Polo took this tradition back home with him to Europe, and eventually it made its way to the New World.

The traditional piñata has seven points, each one representing one of the seven deadly sins. When someone hits the piñata with the stick, they are (symbolically) destroying each of the sins (envy, sloth, gluttony, greed, lust, wrath, and pride), and the candy that spills out symbolizes forgiveness and a fresh new start.

SWEET SERENADES

At Dylan's Candy Bar, candy-themed songs are always playing in the background as people stroll around the aisles—so much more entertaining than your average supermarket canned music! These tunes are also the perfect soundtrack for a sweet soirée for any age.

- "I Want Candy," The Strangegloves, Bow Wow Wow
- "Candyman," Christina Aguilera
- "Honey," Mariah Carey
- "Candy-O," The Cars
- "Sweet Escape," Gwen Stefani

BRAIN CANDY
BIRTHDAY CANDLES

In ancient times, the Greeks offered round cakes adorned with glowing candles to Artemis, the goddess of the moon. They thought the smoke from the candles would reach the gods and carry their wishes and prayers to the heavens. Today, some people are equally superstitious about birthday candles: they believe if you blow them out with one breath, you're in for a year of good luck.

COOKING WITH CANDY: DYLAN'S CANDY BAR CANDY COCKTAILS

For "adults only" parties, these sweet libations from Dylan's Candy Bar are potent!

I SERVING

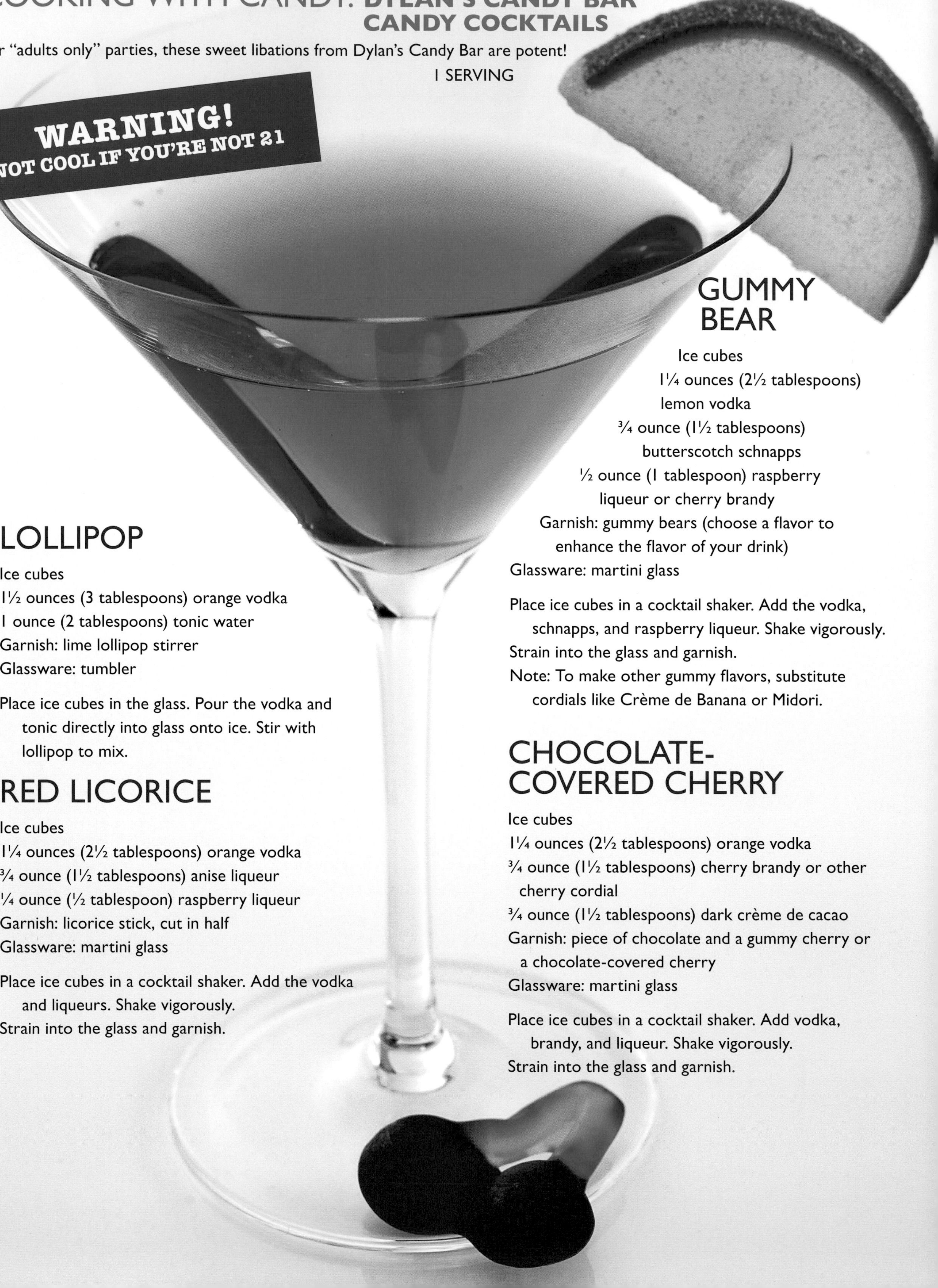

GUMMY BEAR

Ice cubes
1¼ ounces (2½ tablespoons)
lemon vodka
¾ ounce (1½ tablespoons)
butterscotch schnapps
½ ounce (1 tablespoon) raspberry
liqueur or cherry brandy
Garnish: gummy bears (choose a flavor to
enhance the flavor of your drink)
Glassware: martini glass

Place ice cubes in a cocktail shaker. Add the vodka,
schnapps, and raspberry liqueur. Shake vigorously.
Strain into the glass and garnish.
Note: To make other gummy flavors, substitute
cordials like Crème de Banana or Midori.

LOLLIPOP

Ice cubes
1½ ounces (3 tablespoons) orange vodka
1 ounce (2 tablespoons) tonic water
Garnish: lime lollipop stirrer
Glassware: tumbler

Place ice cubes in the glass. Pour the vodka and
tonic directly into glass onto ice. Stir with
lollipop to mix.

RED LICORICE

Ice cubes
1¼ ounces (2½ tablespoons) orange vodka
¾ ounce (1½ tablespoons) anise liqueur
¼ ounce (½ tablespoon) raspberry liqueur
Garnish: licorice stick, cut in half
Glassware: martini glass

Place ice cubes in a cocktail shaker. Add the vodka
and liqueurs. Shake vigorously.
Strain into the glass and garnish.

CHOCOLATE-COVERED CHERRY

Ice cubes
1¼ ounces (2½ tablespoons) orange vodka
¾ ounce (1½ tablespoons) cherry brandy or other
cherry cordial
¾ ounce (1½ tablespoons) dark crème de cacao
Garnish: piece of chocolate and a gummy cherry or
a chocolate-covered cherry
Glassware: martini glass

Place ice cubes in a cocktail shaker. Add vodka,
brandy, and liqueur. Shake vigorously.
Strain into the glass and garnish.

WEDDINGS

SWEET AFFAIRS

Candy is intoxicating, and it can bring out the seductive charm in people. In fact, I've received many letters from candy fans, telling me stories of how candy made them fall in love or how they proposed at Dylan's Candy Bar.

One of the letters I received that touched me most came from a woman named Julie. When she and her husband started dating, they went on a romantic vacation to New York City. They were out to dinner, about to have a "serious" discussion about their future, when Julie glanced out the window of the restaurant and noticed a woman walking by with a Dylan's Candy Bar shopping bag. Not even thinking about the important talk her soon-to-be husband was trying to have with her, Julie blurted out, "Oh, my god, she has a Dylan's Candy Bar bag. That is the best candy store and we have to go there while we are here!"

Then she quickly apologized for getting distracted, and asked him to finish what he was saying. Defeated, he said, "No, don't worry. We'll talk later." Turns out, for the first time he was going to tell her he loved her! Julie wrote to tell me, "From that night on, the phrase 'Dylan's Candy Bar' was code for us to say *'I love you!'*" A year after they married, Julie gave birth to a baby girl, whom they decided to name Dylan because "to us, that means love."

I also enjoyed the story of how a guy proposed to his cupcake-loving girlfriend at my store. He prepped one of our staff to lure her into our café, where cupcakes were being given away. When she approached the table of tasty treats, there, written in the icing, were the words "Will you marry me?"

Another couple, Michelle and David, became the first couple to wed at Dylan's Candy Bar. It was a sweet affair! The wedding party walked down an aisle lined with lollipop trees. The bride's gown—fashioned from Hershey's candy wrappers—was designed for an episode of *Project Runway*. The candy theme even played out in the Chuppah, the traditional Jewish canopy, which—instead of flowers and vines—was decorated with giant lollipops and candy-colored balloons. Wedding guests dined on candy sushi (made of coconut rice, Swedish Fish, and Fruit Roll-Ups) and danced to songs like "Sugar, Sugar."

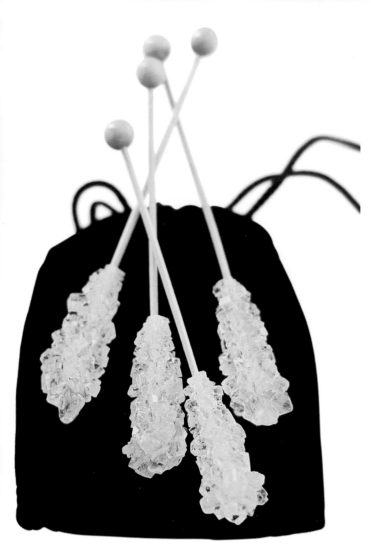

READY TO POP THE QUESTION?

Here are some inspiring ideas based on *actual* proposals made at Dylan's Candy Bar:

● Write your proposal on a plume and place it in a Hershey's Kiss.

● Give her a box of chocolates with the ring as the centerpiece in the box. As she opens the box, get down on one knee.

● Spell out "Marry Me" in colorful pieces of candy or gummy letters.

● Remove the fortunes from fortune cookies. Replace with notes asking her to marry you.

● Insert different names of candy into a candy gram. Use them to describe how each candy reflects your relationship. For instance, Mr. Goodbar or Big Hunk because she caught the hottest bachelor in town; Nutrageous because you're nuts about her; Carefree Gum because she puts you at ease; 100 Grand because having her in your life is better than 100 grand. And so on. Give her the ring last and say that it's for all of the reasons you just mentioned.

● Use her favorite candies to lead her on a trail to you (in a park, in the bedroom, etc.). When she finds you, ask away!

● Put clear rock candy or a Ring Pop in a jewelry box. After she opens it and gets the hint (you hope), give her a real "rock."

● Give her a bouquet of eleven real roses and one made of chocolate. Attach the ring to the chocolate rose's stem.

HOW TO LIVE THE SWEET LIFE WHEN . . .
YOU'RE ALWAYS THE BRIDESMAID, NEVER THE BRIDE

Have faith. Your Mr. Goodbar will come along. But until then, it's up to you to either (a) bemoan your lousy luck in the love department or (b) be the best darn bridesmaid to your friend that you can be. Of course, candy can make the latter a little easier.

BRIDAL SHOWER GAMES

CANDY NECKLACE GAME: When each guest arrives, she receives a Candy Necklace. The guests are instructed *not* to say any of the following words: *wedding, ring, honeymoon, bride,* or *groom* at any point during the shower. If someone does blab any of these bridal terms, the candy necklace is taken away by the guest she said it to. At the shower's end, the one who's acquired the most necklaces wins!

HUGS & KISSES GAME: For a fun twist on a bachelorette game, ask every guy you meet to give the bride-to-be a dollar for a hug and a kiss . . . then arm her with a big bag of Hershey's Hugs & Kisses!

CANDY CRAFT
WEDDING GIFTS

- Create wedding favors with a meaningful twist: attach a dedication to the newlyweds onto a sachet of candies that color-coordinates with the bridesmaids' gowns.

- Make the newlyweds a little care package for their honeymoon flight: monogram carry-on containers and fill with his and her favorite candies.

- Spell out MR. and MRS. on their Welcome Home mat . . . in gummy letters.

- For a housewarming gift, give them candles and bath products scented like chocolate, vanilla, and caramel apple.

- Buy the newlyweds a fondue pot, cupcake tray, or any other cooking supplies that will inspire cooking a romantic dessert for two.

- Give them the wedding gift that keeps on giving (especially if they have sweet tooths): candy-of-the-month club delivery for the year from Dylan's Candy Bar.

CANDY MARRIAGES

Some of the best partnerships exist in candy. Marriages like these last a lifetime:

THIN MINT:
Dark chocolate and creamy mint

BLOW POP:
Bubble gum + lollipop

TOOTSIE POP:
Tootsie Roll + lollipop

BUCKEYES:
Cream + caramel

REESE'S PEANUT BUTTER CUP:
Chocolate + peanut butter

ESPRESSO BEANS:
Coffee bean + chocolate

BRAIN CANDY
WHY IS WHITE CHOCOLATE WHITE?

White chocolate—which is popular for bridal showers and weddings—is made the same way as milk chocolate and dark chocolate; the difference is the ingredients. Plain and dark chocolate are made of cocoa powder, chocolate liquor, cocoa butter, and sugar. Milk chocolate has milk added. White chocolate, however, is made simply of cocoa butter, milk, and sugar. In fact, because there is no chocolate liquor used, many (including the U.S. Food and Drug Administration) don't consider white chocolate to be chocolate at all! It's the cocoa butter that gives it its ivory color and delicate flavor. And because it has a lower melting point than dark chocolate, this creamy confection truly melts in your mouth.

CANDY ICON
WEDDING CAKE

The very first wedding cake wasn't a towering white confection topped with a plastic bride and groom. In fact, it didn't have any icing at all. During the Roman Empire, a loaf of barley bread was baked for the ceremony. The groom would eat some of the bread and break the remaining piece over the bride's head! Guests would then scramble for the crumbs—eating them, they believed, ensured fertility!

In medieval England, small sweet buns were stacked high, then the couple would attempt to kiss over this pile. If the kiss was successful, it was a sign of many kids to come.

In late-nineteenth-century England, the wedding cake was called the bride cake. It was a single-layer plum cake, coated with a white layer of sugar icing. White was a symbol of the "purity" of the bride and also a measure of the couple's wealth. Sugar was expensive, so only the richest could afford a cake this color. In 1859, one of Queen Victoria's daughters was the first bride to have a fancy wedding cake with multilayers and intricate frosting.

CANDY ICONS
JORDAN ALMONDS

In many cultures, Jordan almonds are often given out at monumental occasions: light blue or pink at a christening; red at graduation; green at an engagement party; white at a wedding or silver at a twenty-fifth anniversary. Almonds have a bittersweet taste, which symbolizes life. The sugar coating is added with the hope that the newlyweds' lives will be more sweet than bitter. The egg shape of an almond also symbolizes fertility for the couple.

- In Italy, five Jordan almonds in a pretty box or fabric bag is the most common wedding favor. Each of the five almonds is said to grant the couple a wish for the future: they symbolize health, wealth, fertility, happiness, and longevity.

- At traditional Greek weddings, Jordan almonds are called *koufetta,* and are put into little sachets on a silver tray. The Greeks have long believed that an unmarried woman will dream about her future husband if she sleeps with Jordan almonds beneath her pillow.

- In the Middle East, a Jordan almond is often eaten on the honeymoon night, as they are considered aphrodisiacs!

PETIT FOURS

A petit four is a bite-size, multilayered fancy cake or cookie made of marzipan or pound cake. They are typically served with tea or coffee at the end of a meal (particularly a shower or a wedding). Though itty-bitty, these delicacies are intricately decorated and frosted. The term *petit four* is French and means "low oven." Back in the 1700s, in France, these little cakes were baked in brick ovens after all the other baking was done, to make use of the heat as the ovens cooled down (a "low"-temperature oven).

CANDY CRAFT
BRIDAL TOPIARY

A candy topiary is a unique gift or centerpiece for any occasion. You can theme it by changing the shape or type of candy. For Easter, different colored Peeps can be formed into a flower; for Christmas, foiled chocolate ornaments can be placed into a wreath. For a Valentine's dinner or a creative wedding, chocolate Kisses make for a shimmering floral alternative.

MATERIALS

Small block of floral foam

Clay or plastic flower pot

2½-foot-long dowel (from a hardware store or craft store)

Spray paint in color to match candy

Pumpkin carver or knife

2 Styrofoam balls the size of softballs, or one 1-foot-tall Styrofoam cone

Glue gun or Styrofoam glue

2 13-ounce bags Hershey's Kisses, or any other colorful candy

Toothpicks

Step 1. Place the floral foam block in the pot, leaving 1 inch of clearance at the top.

Step 2. Stick the dowel into the center of the foam inside the pot.

Step 3. Spray-paint the pot and dowel to match the candy theme color.

Step 4. Use the pumpkin carver to cut a hole in the bottom center of each Styrofoam ball that is the width of the dowel, so the balls fit onto the dowel tight enough so they can't slide down. The bottom ball should be a foot from the top of the dowel. The top ball should be at the top of the dowel.

Step 5. With the glue gun or Styrofoam glue, make vertical strips of glue from the center of each ball's bottom to the center of the ball's top. Place Hershey's Kisses base down, next to each other, along the strip.

Step 6. With remaining chocolates, fill in the gaps by inserting a toothpick in the base of a chocolate and inserting the other end into the foam ball. (You can also alternate Kiss colors and angles.)

Step 7. Fill the vase with loose Kisses to cover the foam.

Note: You can cover the pot with a pretty fabric, ribbon, or stickers, or paint on a design.

Lucas

Maggy Siegel

Lauren Volo

CANDY QUIZ
ARE YOU CANDY COMPATIBLE?

You're gaga over Gobstoppers (you like it to last and last and last . . .); your man chomps on sugar-free gum. Does this relationship stand a chance? Take turns taking this quiz, then see if your candy personalities indicate a match or a miss.

1. When you go to the movies you must buy:

(a) A king-size Kit Kat . . . and Sour Patch Kids . . . and a large fountain soda . . . and . . .

(b) Raisinets (at least they sound healthy)

(c) Tic Tacs (if the movie is a bore, you can always entertain your date by shaking the box)

2. If someone gives you a box of chocolates you:

(a) Dive in and devour it

(b) Delicately nibble off a corner of a piece to see what's inside

(c) Pick out the pieces you don't like and regift them to someone in a pretty box

3. Gummy Worms are:

(a) Nature's best creation

(b) Gross

(c) An interesting earring option

4. If you could be any candy you'd be:

(a) A lollipop (the all-day sucker)

(b) An M&M (tidy! "Melts in your mouth, not in your hands!")

(c) A strip of Candy Buttons (after you eat them all off, you have a nice roll of note paper!)

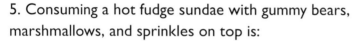

5. Consuming a hot fudge sundae with gummy bears, marshmallows, and sprinkles on top is:

(a) Nirvana

(b) A good reason to never miss your spin class

(c) An artistic and colorful concoction

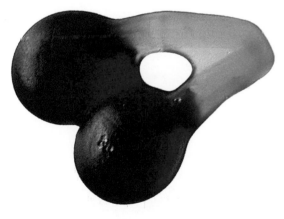

6) When you have a box of Lucky Charms you:

(a) Eat only the marshmallow charms and think they're magically delicious

(b) Eat only the cereal: it has whole grains and vitamin B!

(c) Make a design with the pink hearts, yellow moons, etc.

RATE YOUR ROMANCE

If you chose **MOSTLY A'S,** you're quite a lover (of candy, that is!). You like to indulge yourself in luscious treats and never ever skip dessert. Your only problem is that you sometimes find it hard to share that last bite. Your date might see you as selfish, but you know you're really a sweetheart with a sweet tooth.

If you chose **MOSTLY B'S,** you're scared to unleash your "sweet side." You like treats, but you're afraid of what too much sugar might make you do. What you need is a mate who will comfort you with cotton candy and encourage you to take a bite out of life!

If you chose **MOSTLY C'S,** you have a healthy love of candy and a creative flair that pushes the wrapper. Who knew Dots make a great mosaic for your bedroom? You did! You appreciate a mate who adds spontaneity and flavor to your life. You won't settle for someone with a "vanilla" personality.

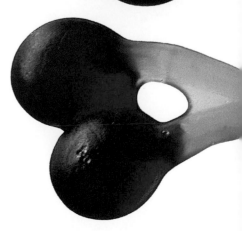

VALENTINE'S DAY

BE MINE

We all know that February 14 is the day to celebrate love with candy. But what you may not know is that the history of Valentine's Day still remains a mystery, making it an even more alluring and seductive holiday! According to one legend, Valentine was a priest in third-century Rome. At the time, Emperor Claudius II forbid all young men to marry; he thought they made better soldiers with no wives to distract them! Valentine thought this was unfair to guys, so he agreed to marry couples on the sly. When Claudius II found out about Valentine's disobedience, he had him put to death.

Another legend portrays Valentine as a prisoner who fell madly in love with the daughter of his jailor. The first "Valentine" was his love letter to her (signed "Your Valentine"), sent shortly before he was put to death. No matter what the story is, Valentine's Day has stuck with us and is one of the most popular holidays, probably because it reminds the world to pay extra attention to loved ones and be sweet.

BRAIN CANDY
VALENTINE'S DAY FUN FACTS

- Most people, single and coupled, dread the pressure of Valentine's Day and think it's "an annoying, commercial holiday." These same people buy Valentine's gifts at the last minute!
- About 15 percent of women send themselves flowers on Valentine's Day.
- Around 3 percent of pet owners prefer to give Valentine's gifts to their pets.

CANDY ICON
HEART BOX OF CHOCOLATES

- More than 36 million heart-shaped boxes of chocolate will be sold for Valentine's Day.
- The first Valentine's Day box of chocolates was introduced by Richard Cadbury, founder of the Cadbury Chocolate Company, in 1868.
- A typical Whitman's Sampler box (the first boxed chocolate to come with a flavor map) contains sixteen flavors of chocolates, including cashew clusters, cherry cordials, Vermont fudge, and vanilla buttercreams.
- The average person takes a bite out of all of the chocolates to get a sense of what they all taste like, and to not feel guilty for eating the entire box.

CANDY ICONS
THE ROSE

Roses have a long history of signifying desire. During the strict Victorian times, couples would use them to communicate their passion secretly. Before you bestow a bouquet on someone—even of the foiled-chocolate variety—consider that every color of a rose has a meaning:

- **RED:** The classic. They symbolize romance and true love.

- **YELLOW:** They mean friendship and freedom. Giving this color signifies a platonic relationship, and no strings attached.

- **PINK:** These are "thank you" roses. They also show happiness and admiration—perhaps the first step in a relationship.

- **ORANGE:** They are the color of the flame and therefore convey passion.

- **WHITE:** They connote innocence, purity, spirituality. White roses can also mean secrecy—as in a secret admirer.

- **LAVENDER:** They convey love at first sight!

CONVERSATION HEARTS

In 1866, the New England Confectionery Company (now Necco Candy Company) first manufactured Conversation Hearts, an iconic and one of the top-selling Valentine's Day candies. Walter Marshall, who developed the sayings, now invents new ones with his grandkids.

About 8 billion Conversation Hearts will be produced this year; that should give you plenty of ways to spell out your feelings. Glue a few onto a card, sneak them in a pocket, or simply place one in a little gift box, tied with a bow. She or he will get the message . . . and you didn't have to say a word!

RED HOTS

Red Hots, Hot Tamales, Atomic Fireballs, and other spicy cinnamon candies are equated with red-hot passion on Valentine's Day. They set your mouth ablaze. But most people say Hot Cinnamon Flaming Hearts actually cause the highest temp on your tongue.

HERSHEY'S KISSES

Hershey's Kisses were introduced in 1907. Supposedly, the candy was named for the sound or motion of the chocolate being deposited onto the conveyor belt during the manufacturing process.

TASTEFUL NICKNAMES

"Candy girl, you are my world . . ."

"Ah sugar, honey honey . . . You are my candy girl . . ."

"Candy . . . I call my sugar candy."

"My Boy, Lollipop!"

Don't hesitate to try out these timeless nicknames on anyone you love. Even some of the most macho rock stars have used them with success.

Bon Bon	Honey	Stud Muffin
Brownie	Hot Cocoa	Sugar
Brown Sugar	Jelly Bean	Sugar Daddy
Buttercup	Ma Cherie ("My	Sugar Muffin
Candy Girl	Sweet" in French)	Sugar Pie
Candy Man	Marshmallow	Sugar Plum
Cookie	Miel ("Honey" in	Sweet Pea
Cuddle Cakes	French)	Sweet Tart
Cupcake	Pop-Tart	Sweetheart
Gummy Bear	Strawberry Shortcake	Sweetie Pie

FAMOUS SWEET NAMES

Check out these lucky celebrities who have some of the sweetest names.

John Candy (late comic actor)

Candy Spelling (related to Tori and Aaron Spelling)

Candy Dulfer (jazz saxophonist)

Sugar Ray Leonard (boxer)

Candy Clark (actress)

Candy Crowley (CNN reporter)

Candy Pratts Price (fashion journalist)

Sugar (Drew Barrymore's character in *Batman Forever*)

HOW TO LIVE THE SWEET LIFE . . .
**WHEN YOU JUST BROKE UP OR DON'T
HAVE A DATE FOR VALENTINE'S DAY**

Moping and feeling sorry for yourself is not an option. Hosting a Chocolate
Movie Marathon is. Send out invites to all of your fellow singletons and
instruct them to BYOC (bring your own chocolate). And remember—
calories don't count on Valentine's Day.

Why not screen:

Chocolat

Like Water for Chocolate

Willy Wonka and the Chocolate Factory

Charlie and the Chocolate Factory

Forrest Gump ("Life is like a box of chocolates . . .")

E.T. (even aliens like chocolate)

If you're really bitter on this holiday, show *Psycho* (chocolate syrup was used
to simulate blood in the famous shower scene!). If your friends swear by
gummies, or are worried men prefer "pixie sticks," then here are some
low-cal alternatives: *Strangers with Candy, Jawbreaker, Hard Candy, Candy.*

BRAIN CANDY
CHOCOLATE: AN APHRODISIAC

Every boy should be taught at an early age that the real way to a woman's heart is through chocolate. (In fact, "some women would rather fall in chocolate than in love!") Besides being sweet, candy can also be sexy . . . and seductive. I learned this lesson in the first grade, when I fell, head over sneakers, for the boy who revealed his secret crush on me with a classic heart box of chocolates. One bite of that vanilla-cream–filled confection and, well, I was smitten.

Across the map, throughout history, chocolate has long been thought of as an aphrodisiac. The Aztecs associated chocolate with Xochiquetzal, their goddess of fertility. They thought that chocolate invigorated men and made women less inhibited. Montezuma, king of the Aztecs, believed that eating chocolate would make him a more lusty (and powerful!) lover.

In 1624, Johan Franciscus Rauch, a Viennese professor, insisted chocolate be banned from monasteries; he feared it was "an inflamer of passions." Madame du Barry, Louis XV's mistress, also believed in its seductive powers: she served her loves this "elixir of love" in a cup before luring them into her bedroom. Physicians in the 1800s prescribed chocolate to suppress the desires of lovesick patients. And the ultimate lover, Casanova, consumed the sweet stuff to kick-start romance.

There is a scientific reason chocolate makes you feel so good—and "in the mood." It contains two "love chemicals," phenylethylamine and serotonin, both of which are found naturally in the brain. These substances are released into the nervous system when you feel happy—and also when you feel love or lust. It gives an instant energy boost, increases stamina, and like love, some say it is addictive. In a nutshell, consuming chocolate can make you feel euphoric.

Some chocoholics claim that consuming chocolate makes their whole body flush. If you've ever sunk your teeth into a decadent Belgian chocolate truffle, you'll understand. So knowing that chocolate has the power to ignite passion, I'd suggest using this natural wonder drug to your advantage (and not just on February 14). Breakfast, lunch, dinner—every meal can inspire passion. At breakfast, why not sprinkle some chocolate chips into pancakes? Even drizzle chocolate fudge on fresh fruit! Add cocoa to your regular coffee and make it a mocha. Or bake chocolate chip cookies from scratch with a loved one—and eat them under the covers!

CANDY QUIZ

ARE YOU A CHOCOHOLIC?

Sure, you love chocolate and you occasionally crave it. But chocoholics—in the true sense—are a rare and proud breed. They eat, sleep, and breathe this delectable confection. They would rather give up alcohol, sex, reading tabloids, going on Facebook, even shopping, than surrender their daily fix. Not sure if you're ready to join the ranks? If you answer yes to more than five of the following, you're well on your way.

❑ Every night, visions of sugar plums dipped in fudge dance in my head.

❑ I am a member of The World Chocolate Society: in October, I fly to Paris for the Chocolate Salon; in November, I taste everything at the New York Chocolate Show; and every February, I road-trip to the Annual Chocolate Lovers Festival in Fairfax, Virginia.

❑ I have sampled all of the following: truffles with real gold shavings; bacon-flavored chocolate bars; even chocolate-covered ants!

❑ My favorite color is chocolate brown; close second is mocha.

❑ I've consumed the entire 2-pound milk chocolate Dylan's Candy Bar in one sitting.

❑ I subscribe to the twelve-step chocoholic program: "Never be more than 12 steps away from a piece!"

I ABIDE BY ALL OF THESE SWEET SAYINGS:

❑ "There's nothing better than a good friend—except a good friend with chocolate."

❑ "Once you consume chocolate, chocolate will consume you."

❑ "Anything tastes better dipped in chocolate."

❑ "Money talks. Chocolate sings!"

❑ "Chocolate is nature's way of making up for Mondays."

❑ "Coffee makes it possible to get out of bed, but chocolate makes it worthwhile."

❑ "Seven days without chocolate makes one weak."

❑ "Forget diamonds! Chocolate is a girl's best friend."

❑ "Coffee, chocolate, men—some things are better rich!"

BRAIN CANDY
CHOCOLATE FUN FACTS

- Americans spend more than $7 billion on chocolate and consume about 2.8 billion pounds of it yearly!

- The average American eats 10 to 12 pounds (about 27,000 calories worth!) of chocolate a year. The average Swiss eats 27 pounds a year (okay, they win!).

- According to Pat Kendall, Ph.D., a Food Science and Nutrition Specialist at Colorado State University, chocolate is the most commonly craved food in North America; 40 percent of American women and 15 percent of American men are "chocoholics."

- According to *The Guinness Book of World Records*, the largest chocolate bar weighed 7,892 pounds, 8 ounces, and was made by Elah Dufour-Novi in Alessandria, Piemonte, Italy, on October 11, 2007.

- In 2008, to celebrate the launch of Thorntons Moments chocolates, the UK company created the world's largest box of chocolates. It was 16.5 feet tall, 11.5 feet wide, and contained 220,000 individually wrapped pieces of chocolate!

- MarieBelle in New York City sold (and may still take special custom orders for) the world's most expensive box of chocolates. For $15,000 you can purchase the Chocolate Picnic Steamer Trunk containing 500 pieces of chocolate ganache, 5 pounds of chocolate bark and croquettes, 80 ounces of Aztec hot chocolate, 8 ounces of Aztec Hot Chocolate Bars, and Aztec Iced Chocolate. It also comes with a leather journal, a teapot, an infuser, and a small library filled with books about chocolate!

- Lovers express their lust by giving green M&M's (they are rumored to be an aphrodisiac). On Valentine's Day, M&M's/Mars even sells them solo as "the color of love." The green M&M is the only female, and the seductress of the M&M's characters.

- Artist Luis Morera and Chocovic, the largest chocolate producer in Spain, created a 7-metric-ton chocolate heart for Valentine's Day 2002. The grand confection was commissioned by online dating service Match.com and made it into the *Guinness Book of World Records*.

A CHOCOLATE A DAY CAN KEEP THE DOCTOR AWAY!

- Studies have shown that consuming a small bar of dark chocolate every day can reduce blood pressure in individuals with high blood pressure.

- Dark chocolate has been shown to reduce LDL cholesterol (the bad cholesterol) by up to 10 percent.

- Dark chocolate is a potent antioxidant. Antioxidants gobble up free radicals, destructive molecules that are implicated in heart disease and other ailments.

- Chocolate contains the neurotransmitter serotonin, which acts as an antidepressant.

- Chocolate is a great energy source! A single chocolate chip can provide enough energy for an adult to walk 150 feet.

BRAIN CANDY
FONDUE

Fondue stems from the French word *fondre,* which means "to melt." Originally, people in Switzerland made cheese fondue in a large communal pot as a way of using up dry, hardened cheese. In the 1950s, cheese and chocolate fondue made their way to the United States and became an elegant dessert option and a fad for parties. Chocolate fondue is a warm, sweet chocolate sauce that you dip treats into—everything from fruit and cake to nuts, marshmallows, bread, even whole chiles. Be creative: anything tastes better dipped in chocolate! Break out the double boiler or a pretty fondue pot and start melting. Note: Look, chocoholics, even the bottle is really foiled chocolate.

COOKING WITH CANDY

DYLAN'S CANDY BAR DELECTABLE FONDUE

Serves 4 or more

1¼ cups heavy cream
1 pound good-quality bittersweet chocolate, finely chopped
1 tablespoon vanilla extract

Heat the cream in a small, heavy saucepan over moderate heat just until it comes to a bare simmer. Add the chocolate and let stand for 2 minutes. Add the vanilla and whisk until smooth. Serve immediately. Note: Use a skewer or fondue fork so you don't burn your fingers.

Skinny fondue: Use ½ cup unsweetened cocoa powder, ¼ cup granulated sugar, 2 tablespoons Splenda, ½ cup skim evaporated milk, and 1½ teaspoons vanilla extract.

Caramel fondue: Instead of chocolate, melt 2 bags of mini caramels.

Red Hot fondue: Add 1 tablespoon cinnamon and ½ teaspoon chili powder.

Nutty fondue: Add some chopped pecans, almonds, walnuts, and hazelnuts. Or, stir in ⅔ cup creamy peanut butter.

Charged-up fondue: Sprinkle in 1 tablespoon instant coffee granules. Or pour in ½ cup hot brewed coffee or espresso.

Naughty fondue: Pour in 1 to 2 tablespoons of your favorite liqueur or brandy to up the ante.

WARNING! NOT COOL IF YOU'RE NOT 21 ↑

COOKING WITH CANDY

PRETTY 'N PINK FROZEN MOUSSE

Serves 2

2 cups whipping cream, cold
1¼ cups confectioners' sugar
1 pint strawberries, washed and mashed
Candy toppings: Conversation Hearts, Red Hots, and marshmallows
Pink chocolate roses

Whip the cream until thick. Gradually beat in the confectioners' sugar, a little at a time. Fold in the mashed strawberries. Spread in an 8-inch square dish (or mold) and freeze until firm. Top with candy and garnish with a chocolate rose.

HOW TO LIVE THE SWEET LIFE WHEN ...
YOUR LOVE LIFE NEEDS SOME SPARKS

You know you love each other, but sometimes you run out of fresh, exciting ways to express it. Candy adds instant amoré!

- Play the following risqué songs: "Candy Shop" by Madonna; "Candy Shop" by Fifty Cent; "Candy" by Snoop Dog; "Sugar" by Trick Daddy; "Pour Some Sugar on Me" by Def Leppard.

- Break out the flavored edible body paint, and find your inner artists.

- Make warm chocolate soufflé for dessert and feed it to each other.

- Blindfold your partner and feed him or her different chocolate candies. Have him or her guess what they are.

- Curl up by a fireplace and roast s'mores (be sure to clean each other's fingers with your lips!).

- Breakfast in bed for no occasion is a total turn-on. Serve him or her chocolate chip pancakes with white-chocolate–covered strawberries and Champagne.

- Create your own sweet spa at home. Take turns massaging each other with candy-scented creams.

- Don edible lingerie or eat chocolate naked. End of story.

EASTER

HONEY BUNNY

My candy obsession has only one rival—my love for rabbits. I have more than 3,000 rabbit items in my collection, from stuffed animals, plates, and stationery to hand towels and cookie jars. They definitely seem to multiply in my house! My rabbit collection started when I was three years old, when my dad brought back a pink stuffed Steiff rabbit from Europe. This bunny was taller than I was—to me, it was literally larger than life. I would drag it everywhere by its arms, until the cotton filling started to tear through. At that point, my mom gave me "the baby" of this rabbit—a mini plush version that was much easier to carry around. I slept with it every night.

However, the best addition to my rabbit collection came from my parents when I was nine: two real pet bunnies. One was black and one was white, both with silky fur and cute, soulful brown eyes. I immediately named them Chocolate and Vanilla (ironic, right?). And oddly enough, they even shared my love for sweets. It was Oreos—not typical bunny food like lettuce or carrots—that enabled me to lure them from their grassy pen into their cages at night.

I have honored my pet rabbits Chocolate and Vanilla by making them the Dylan's Candy Bar Mascots. Chocolate the Bunny is a 10-foot rabbit sculpture covered in candy foil and looks like it's made of real chocolate. Customers often pose for pictures with him and then try to eat him, since he seems quite edible. Chocolate and Vanilla have become paraphernalia for my company, in plush, T-shirts, lollipops, and chocolate figurines.

To me, and as evident in Dylan's Candy Bar and many other entertainment and advertising companies, rabbits are more than just synonymous with Easter. Bunnies can embody so many different personalities, from wild and wacky (Bugs Bunny, Trix Rabbit) to graceful, sexy, and seductive (Jessica Rabbit and the ever-famous Playboy Bunny!). In many cultures, rabbits usher in good luck. They also represent happiness, energy, speed, resilience, and springtime, and they serve as a reminder to always maintain a youthful spirit and have a spring in your step.

CANDY ICON
CHOCOLATE BUNNY

More than 60 million chocolate Easter bunnies are produced each year. The first edible ones were made in Germany in the early 1800s. Though these bunnies range in size and weight (one of the tallest is 3 feet and 75 pounds), people still devour the entire cute creation. According to the NCA, 76 percent of Americans believe you should bite a chocolate bunny's ears first, 5 percent said bunnies should be eaten feet first, while 4 percent favored eating the tail first.

BRAIN CANDY
THE EASTER RABBIT

Since ancient times, the rabbit has been a symbol of fertility and birth. But the first written mentions of the Easter Bunny come from Germany in the 1500s. German settlers brought the tradition of the Easter Bunny to Pennsylvania, and called him Osterhase, or Oschter Haws. The night before Easter, he would distribute brightly colored eggs into the special nests that good children made to decorate their caps and bonnets. Eventually, the bunny brought chocolate and candies as well as eggs, and left his treats in decorated Easter baskets all over the United States.

BRAIN CANDY
WORLD FAMOUS BUNNIES

- Peter Cottontail, aka the Easter Bunny
- Brer Rabbit, from Disney's *Song of the South*
- Bugs Bunny, "What's up, Doc?" Warner Bros. cartoon rabbit
- The Trix Rabbit, "Silly rabbit, Trix are for kids!"
- Jessica Rabbit and Roger Rabbit, from *Who Framed Roger Rabbit?*
- The Energizer Bunny, "He keeps on going . . . and going . . . and going."
- Thumper, from *Bambi*
- The White Rabbit and March Hare, from *Alice's Adventures in Wonderland*
- Rabbit, from *Winnie-the-Pooh*
- Peter Rabbit, created by British author Beatrix Potter
- The Nestlé Quik Bunny, a great way to sweeten milk!
- The Velveteen Rabbit, the stuffed animal that comes alive through the love of its owner

- It's Happy Bunny, the mischievous character created by Jim Benton that says sardonic stuff like, "When life gives you lemons, squirt juice into your enemy's eyes!"
- Miffy, the little female bunny in Dick Bruna's Dutch picture books; and a kids' TV show on Noggin
- Felix the Rabbit, a French stuffed animal that travels the world to find home
- Oswald the Lucky Rabbit, the cartoon character co-created by Walt Disney for Universal Pictures in the 1920s
- My Melody, Hello Kitty's bunny pal
- The Playboy Bunny, Hugh Hefner's playmate
- Harvey, the invisible rabbit in the Jimmy Stewart movie
- Max and Ruby, brother and sister bunnies on Nickelodeon

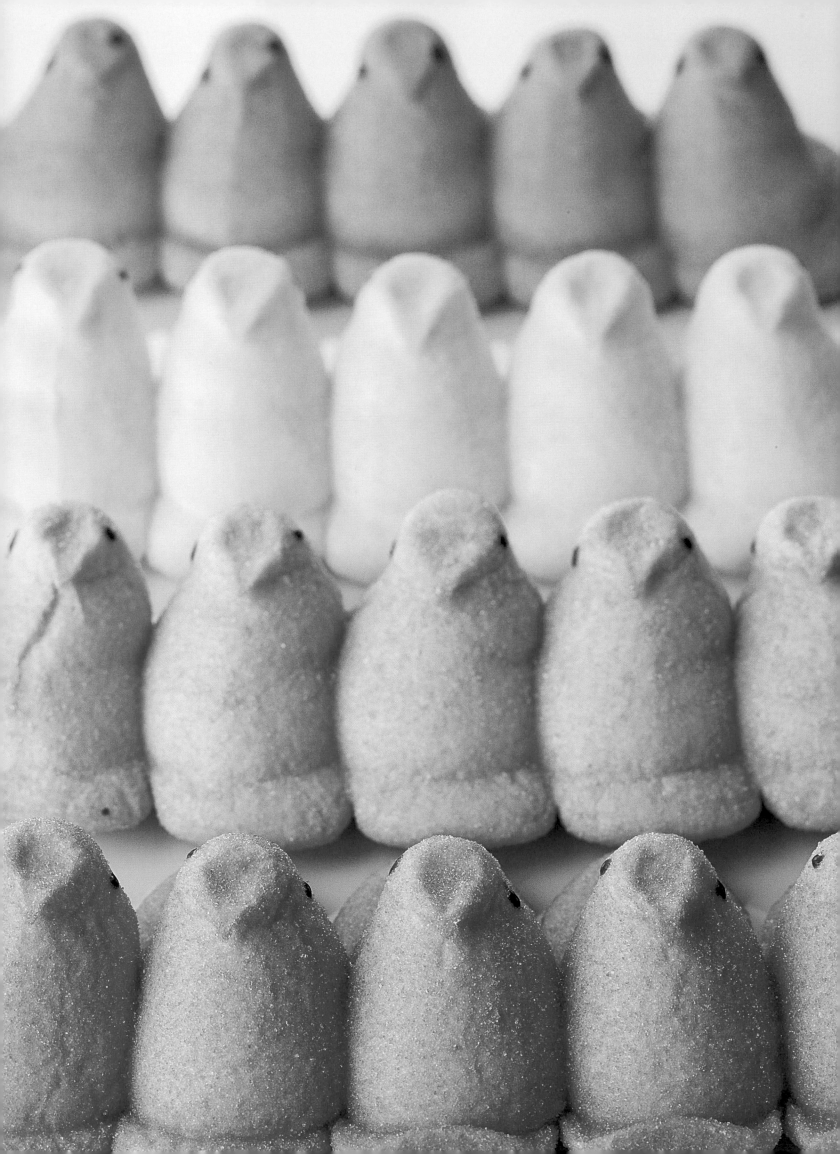

ENTERTAINING WITH CANDY
SPRING FAVORITES

While the Easter Rabbit is the major symbol for Easter candy, chicks and lambs are definitely adored in candy form. Tulips and eggs are also prevalent. Any of these candies, whether in foiled chocolate, dextrose, or gummy form, make for festive spring decor. Grass place mats covered with chicks and eggs, or vases filled with fresh chocolate tulips, will enliven your home.

CANDY ICON
PEEPS

In 1946, the Just Born Candy Company bought the Rodda Candy Company and inherited its molds for making marshmallow chicks. In 1953, a single marshmallow Peep took more than a full day—27 hours in all—to create. That's a far cry from today's time to produce one: from start to finish, 6 minutes.

Just Born's Bethlehem, Pennsylvania, factory produces more than 1 billion Peeps a year—that works out to about 4 million Peeps a day! While most people eat Peeps straight out of the package, fans say you can serve them up several other ways: microwaved, frozen, roasted, and even as the topping on a pizza.

CHOCOLATE EGGS

One of my absolute favorite Easter items to use in baskets or to recommend that people use for decorating are foiled chocolate eggs. I love all the colors they come in. And the way they pop on the table—especially on fake grass. Chocolate eggs are also very popular for the Easter hunt. Some families place a value on the different colors. The winner of the hunt is the one who accumulates the majority of the most valuable colors.

Candy companies also make very beautiful decorative foils for their chocolate eggs. I recommend making a spring bouquet or centerpiece using these. It's a nice alternative to the Easter basket.

COOKING WITH CANDY **SWEET EATS FOR SPRING**

Celebrate the warm weather that's finally here with these two great recipes. Just what the doctor ordered for "spring fever."

BUNNY COOKIES

Makes 3 dozen cookies

2¾ cups all-purpose flour

1 teaspoon baking soda

½ teaspoon baking powder

¼ teaspoon salt

2 sticks (1 cup) unsalted butter, softened

1½ cups sugar

1 large egg

1 teaspoon vanilla extract

One 3½-inch rabbit-shaped cookie cutter (or chicks, flowers, and other springtime shapes for variety)

1 store-bought container vanilla or strawberry frosting

Assorted candies, for decorating

Whisk together the flour, baking soda, baking powder, and salt in a medium bowl. Set aside.

In a large bowl with an electric mixer, beat together the butter and sugar until pale and fluffy. Beat in the egg and vanilla. Add the flour mixture gradually and mix on low speed just until combined. Form dough into two 5-inch disks. Wrap each in plastic wrap and chill until firm, at least 2 hours or overnight.

Preheat the oven to 375°F and line two cookies sheets with parchment paper. Working with one disk at a time (keep remaining disk chilled), remove plastic wrap and roll the dough on a well-floured surface with a floured rolling pin into a 16-inch round between ⅛ and ¼ inch thick. Cut out as many cookies as possible with cutters and transfer to prepared cookie sheets, placing the cutouts 1 inch apart. Bake in upper and lower thirds of the oven until the tops are golden, switching pans halfway through baking, 8 to 10 minutes total, and then cool cookies for 2 minutes on pan. Transfer cookies with a metal spatula to racks to cool completely.

Gather scraps and chill until firm enough to reroll in the same manner. Make more cookies with the remaining dough and scraps (reroll once) in same manner on cooled baking sheets. Frost and top cookies decoratively with assorted candies.

DIRT CAKE

Serves up to 6 people (1 cup each)

1 (9 ounce) package chocolate sandwich cookies

2 tablespoons unsalted butter, softened

1 (8 ounce) package cream cheese, softened

1 cup confectioners' sugar

1 (5.9 ounce) box chocolate instant pudding

1¾ cups whole milk

1 (8 ounce) tub whipped cream

1 small package chocolate-covered raisins

6 gummy worms

6 flower lollipops

Pulse the cookies in a food processor until finely ground, and set aside. Beat the butter, cream cheese, and sugar in a large bowl with an electric mixer until smooth and fluffy. In a medium bowl, whisk together the pudding mix and milk until incorporated. Whisk the whipped cream into the pudding mixture until smooth, then beat into the butter mixture in a large bowl until combined well.

To assemble, fill six (1½-cup capacity) clear glasses each with 2 tablespoons of ground cookies, then ½ cup each of filling mixture, and 2 more tablespoons of cookie crumbs. Then top evenly with remaining filling mixture and end with remaining cookie crumbs. Top each decoratively with a few chocolate-covered raisins for rocks, a gummy worm, and a flower lollipop.

CANDY CRAFT
EGG-SQUISITE CREATION 1: CHERRY BLOSSOMS

Step 1. Put 20 eggs into the vase to weigh it down.

Step 2. Stick the branches into the vase.

Step 3. Cut 20 pieces of ribbon each 1½ feet long.

Step 4. Tape an individual egg to the bottom inch of each piece of ribbon.

Step 5. Tie the other end of each ribbon to the branches at varying lengths.

Step 6. Display as a table centerpiece or a pretty alternative to flowers.

MATERIALS

40 chocolate eggs in pastel colors (preferably flat lightweight ones)

Vase

Real or fake cherry blossom branches (or any branch with buds of a spring flower)

30 yards satin ¼-inch-wide ribbon in varying pastel colors

Masking tape

Scissors

CANDY CRAFT
EGG-SQUISITE CREATION 2: WAFER EGG

Step 1. Rest the pointy side of the Styrofoam egg on the plastic cup rim to steady the egg.

Step 2. Put a drop of glue on a Necco wafer and adhere to the bottom of the egg.

Step 3. Cover ¼ of the flat part of that Necco wafer with a second wafer in a different color.

Step 4. Cover ¼ of the right part of the second Necco wafer with a third wafer in a different color. Continue horizontally overlapping ¼ of the wafer until the row is complete.

Step 5. Following the same steps, start another row of wafers. Once all rows are completed and dry, carefully turn the egg over and rest onto the cup with the bottom side down.

Step 6. Finish covering the rest of egg in horizontal overlapping rows.

Step 7. Tie a ribbon around the egg and display proudly on an egg cup.

MATERIALS

Styrofoam egg and plastic cup

Styrofoam glue or glue gun

8 packs Necco wafers

Ribbon

CANDY ICONS
PANORAMIC SUGAR EGG

Panoramic sugar eggs were a Victorian Easter tradition. These are made from molded sugar and are elaborately decorated with pastel royal icing. One end of the hollow egg has a peephole; tucked inside is an intricate miniature sugar icing scene.

JORDAN ALMONDS

This egg-shaped candy comes in beautiful pastel shades. It is served at Easter to represent rebirth and fertility; the pretty colors also brighten a spring table.

CANDY ICON
JELLY BEANS

One of the bestselling candies for every day and for Easter is the jelly bean. According to the National Confectioners Association, U.S. manufacturers produce more than 16 billion jelly beans for Easter each year. In the early 1900s, jelly beans were a popular penny candy item as well as the first "bulk candy," one of the first sweets to be sold by weight. Experts believe that the jelly bean descended from Turkish delight, a popular Middle Eastern confection in biblical times. In the 1930s, jelly beans became considered an Easter candy—probably due to their pretty bright colors and egglike shape. The Easter Bunny delivers them as a symbol of new life in the springtime.

Opposite: Those gigantic jelly beans are filled with marshmallow and called hen eggs.

CANDY CRAFT
EASTER BASKET

Step 1. Using the vessel of your choice, measure the base and cut a piece of corrugated board so that it fits snugly into the basket. The corrugated board should stick out 10 to 12 inches from the upper rim of the vessel.

Step 2. Sink the corrugated board into the center of the basket, then with decorative shredded paper (or other filler), stuff the shred in front and behind the board so there is enough shred in the bucket to support the board.

Step 3. After selecting the candies for the basket, divide the candies by size, shape, and weight. Ideally, you should divide candies into three categories: light, heavy, and filler—for example, candy bars are flat and light, a tube of hot chocolate is heavy and awkwardly shaped, and lollipops (because they are generally small) are used as filler.

Step 4. Gather the light candies and begin taping them to the corrugated board. Line the outer rim of the corrugated board with the candy and work your way in, putting the lighter candies toward the back and the heavier toward the front, piling each product on top of the next. This helps to anchor the weight so that the board does not lean backward. Any product you have selected as filler will be used to put in wherever there are gaps between candies.

Step 5. When you are pleased with how your candies have been arranged, take a cellophane bag and place the basket in the center of the bag. With scissors, snip the bottom two corners of the bag to allow for air to flow through when tying the bow. Pinch the top of the cellophane in the center above the basket and gather the remainder of the cello into your hands to form a gathering.

Step 6. Using a piece of sturdy ribbon, tie the bundle of cello and make a double knot. Pull the excess cello from the top to smooth out the bag. Cut approximately an inch off the top, so that the bunching is uniform, and fan it out. Where you previously cut air pockets, fold the cellophane inward toward the basket and tape (do this on both sides). Tape any excess cello directly to the bottom of the vessel.

Step 7. Tie a piece of silk ribbon at the length of your choice (it should fall halfway down the basket). Tie it around your previous ribbon. Then, using about six different colors of curling ribbon, measure out an arm's length of the ribbon (repeat twice). Tie a simple bow around your silk ribbon, trim off any excess, and voilà, you're done!

TOOLS & MATERIALS

1 large pastel wicker basket or vessel of your choice

1 piece white corrugated board to fit in basket or vessel of choice

1 bag cellophane or paper crinkle in grass green

Large clear cellophane bag

Scissors

Sturdy ribbon

Clear packing tape or glue gun

Silk ribbon

6 colors of curling ribbon

SUGGESTED CANDIES:

- 1 (1- to 3-pound) box chocolate truffles (splurge on the best Belgian ones if you're trying to win brownie points)

- 3 assorted chocolate bars with colorful wrappers (you can tie them together with a pretty ribbon)

- 1 bag assorted foiled chocolate eggs or colorful marshmallow hen eggs

- 1 mini pail or Chinese take-out box

- ½ pound Easter candy corn

- ½ pound loose jelly beans

- Large foiled chocolate bunny (you can also do a large plush bunny and use smaller chocolate bunnies around it)

- 6 Easter sugar cookies

- 4 to 6 Easter lollipops

- 10-count box of Peeps

- Bag of colored popcorn

- Box of jelly beans

FOURTH OF JULY

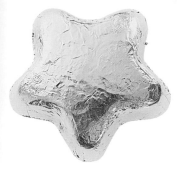

THE UNITED STATES OF CANDY

Even when the economy looks grim, there is one thing for certain that is recession-proof: candy! During the Great Depression, World Wars, and subsequent recessions, chocolate and candy sales remained strong. For example, in 2007, despite the economic crisis and while other industries' sales were down, candy was up about 3 percent from the year before. Americans spent $29 billion on candy! So why, even when we're tightening our belts, are we still digging into the candy jar?

Simple. Candy is one of the rare items on the planet that is inexpensive and completely enjoyable! It is a vice that's too affordable to give up—a "happy meal" that provides enough energy and sustenance, and a product that appeals to a wider demographic than most. Candy is a comfort food that reminds people of "the good ol' days." It's a flashback to a simpler time, when life was easier, sweeter, more predictable. When you're hungry for those days, it's easy enough to choose a childhood favorite or bite into a nostalgic candy, like a Charleston Chew or Abba Zabba.

The Nostalgia Department at Dylan's Candy Bar is extremely popular during tough times. Baby boomers seek the retro candy and vintage logo T-shirts, lunch boxes, and stationery, viewing it as holding onto a piece—literally—of American history. When shopping on eBay or at antiques shows, I'm always surprised by how in demand vintage candy paraphernalia becomes when the economy is shaky. Gumball machines from 1950s diners, Uncle Sam Pez dispensers, Bazooka Joe T-shirts from the 1970s, and Hershey's tin advertisements from the 1950s increase in value sometimes triplefold.

Candy can help revive our patriotism and faith in the future. It is a part of America's heritage. We produce and have been importing sugar for centuries. Annually, the United States imports over $800 million of cane sugar and beet sugar from around the world. Many of our country's great candy pioneers are proof of the possibility of the American dream. Some were immigrants to America; many grew up in small American towns. Yet they turned their sweet dreams into million- and billion-dollar businesses.

Milton Hershey was born on a Pennsylvania farm and started his own candy business at age nineteen, in Philadelphia. His vision was

not just to create a thriving business, but to also support his local community of dairy farmers. Their supply of fresh milk allowed him to mass-produce his milk chocolate products, and he in turn helped them create a booming town filled with homes, parks, and recreation. That town, of course, became known as Hershey, a favorite vacation destination for candy lovers!

Another candy entrepreneur, William Wrigley Jr., was born in Pennsylvania in 1861. His parents were second-generation Americans, and Wrigley worked in his dad's soap business for twenty years before deciding it was time to try his own fortune. With $32 in his pocket, he borrowed $5,000 from his uncle (with the provision that his cousin become his partner) to start a chewing-gum business. The company was a huge success, mainly owing to Wrigley's promotional savvy. In 2008, the Mars Candy Company acquired Wrigley—when the company's worth was estimated at $23 billion.

Mars began in 1911 as the Mar-O-Bar Company, a snack food business founded by Frank C. Mars of Tacoma, Washington, who whipped up buttercream candy in his home. In 1920, he moved to a larger factory in Minneapolis, where the Snickers and Milky Way bars were created. The company continues to develop great products, such as Twix, Three Musketeers bars, and M&M's.

I take great pride in our United States of Candy and the candy pioneers who forged this industry. I think we can all learn a lesson from them, and also from former president Ronald Reagan, who used to hand out jelly beans at his cabinet meetings. There's not a crisis that candy can't help solve—or at least make seem a whole lot easier to swallow!

BRAIN CANDY
CANDY CLASSICS

According to Candyfavorites.com, approximately 65 percent of American candy bar brands have been around for longer than sixty years.

CANDY QUIZ
SUGARY SLOGANS

Sure, these slogans sound familiar. But can you recall which sweet was the subject of these catchy ad campaigns? Check your answers (no treat if you cheat!) below.

1. "It's too good for kids."

2. "Makes mouths happy."

3. "Isn't life juicy?"

4. "Don't let hunger happen to you."

5. "Sometimes you feel like a nut. Sometimes you don't."

6. "Crispety, crunchety, peanut-buttery . . ."

7. "Double your pleasure, double your fun."

8. "Gimme a break."

9. "Get the sensation."

10. "It's more than a mouthful, it's . . ."

11. "Taste the Rainbow . . ."

12. "You got your chocolate in my peanut butter . . ."

Answers: 1. Toffifay. 2. Twizzlers. 3. Starburst. 4. Snickers. 5. Mounds and Almond Joy. 6. Butterfinger. 7. Doublemint Gum. 8. Kit-Kat. 9. York Peppermint Patty. 10. Whatchamacallit. 11. Skittles. 12. Reese's Peanut Butter Cups.

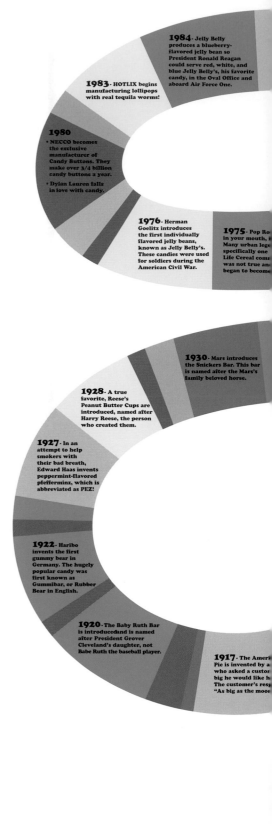

1984. Jelly Belly produces a blueberry-flavored jelly bean so President Ronald Reagan could serve red, white, and blue Jelly Belly's, his favorite candy, in the Oval Office and aboard Air Force One.

1983. HOTLIX begins manufacturing lollipops with real tequila worms!

1980
• NECCO becomes the exclusive manufacturer of Candy Buttons. They make over 3/4 billion candy buttons a year.
• Dylan Lauren falls in love with candy.

1976. Herman Goelitz introduces the first individually flavored jelly beans, known as Jelly Belly's. These candies were used for soldiers during the American Civil War.

1975. Pop Ro in your mouth, Many urban lege specifically one Life Cereal comm was not true and began to become

1930. Mars introduces the Snickers Bar. This bar is named after the Mars's family beloved horse.

1928. A true favorite, Reese's Peanut Butter Cups are introduced, named after Harry Reese, the person who created them.

1927. In an attempt to help smokers with their bad breath, Edward Haas invents peppermint-flavored pfefferminz, which is abbreviated as PEZ!

1922. Haribo invents the first gummy bear in Germany. The hugely popular candy was first known as Gummibar, or Rubber Bear in English.

1920. The Baby Ruth Bar is introduced and is named after President Grover Cleveland's daughter, not Babe Ruth the baseball player.

1917. The Ameri Pie is invented by a who asked a custor big he would like h The customer's resp "As big as the moo

100,000 BC. Cavemen's first known craving for sweets is honey in the beehive. "Me love sweets."

2000 BC. Egyptians combine the marshmallow root with honey, forming the first real candy, the marshmallow. This was used only for gods and royalty.

1993 - The first [ro]tating pop is [in]vented, called [th]e Spin Pop.

2001 - Dylan Lauren opens her flagship store in Manhattan called Dylan's Candy Bar.

2003 - Dylan Lauren expands her stores to Long Island, Florida, and Texas.

2008 - Dylan's Candy Bar expands from 10,000 to 15,000 square feet and three floors!

1954
• Just Born mechanizes the Peep-making process, cutting the creation time from 27 hours per Peep to 6 minutes!

• Dubble-Bubble began sponsoring bubble-gum-blowing contests, which became so popular they were eventually televised.

1953 - Bazooka changes its packaging and adds a small comic strip featuring the character Bazooka Joe.

1960
• Ferrera Pan introduces Lemon Heads, shortly followed by Apple, Grape, and Orange Heads.

• M&M Mars introduces Starbursts in England in an attempt to make healthy candy. It didn't come to the United States until 1976.

1958 - Candy Necklaces are introduced.

1961 - Sam Born invents a machine that mechanically inserts sticks into lollipops.

1952 - Pez Candy is introduced to the United States. The first dispensers were Santa Claus and a Robot.

1950 - A Catholic priest invents a machine to mass-produce candy canes.

1932
• Mars introduces the 3 Musketeers Bar, named after its usage of 3 different flavors of nougat. In 1945 the recipe was changed to only chocolate nougat.

• Ferrera Pan introduces Red Hots.

1934 - L. Frutola, which later is called Lik M Aid, accidently becomes a candy. Its original purpose was a drink mix. Pixy Stix shortly follows in straw form.

1940 - The board game Candy Land is invented to keep sick children entertained.

1941 - M&M's Plain Chocolate Candies are introduced. Years later the name is changed to M&M's.

1949 - Smarties, often referred to as candy pills, are invented by a British gentleman in his rented New Jersey garage.

[ro]tsie Pop, [is] combine two [is] invented.

1907 - Hershey's invents the Chocolate Kiss. It was named the Kiss because the machine that made them looked like it was kissing the conveyor belt.

1906 - The first bubble gum invented is called Blibber Blubber. However, the gum was never marketed; its texture resembled Silly Putty. Year's later, it is perfected and renamed Double Bubble.

1912 - The Life Saver, which is named after its ring shape, is introduced in its signature peppermint flavor. Twenty-two years later, the fruit flavors are introduced to mass market.

1913 - The Goo Goo Cluster is created and is the first bar to include milk chocolate, caramel, marshmallows, and peanuts.

1904 - Cotton Candy, known then as Fairy Floss, is introduced at the St. Louis World's Fair. The most popular color of cotton candy is pink.

• Mary Janes, made of peanut butter and molasses, are invented by the Miller Family. They name the candy after Charles Miller's favorite aunt.

1914
• The American Licorice Company produces its first licorice candy, later creating Red Vines. Licorice root was originally used over 3,000 years ago for cough and cold remedies.

1898 - Beeman's gum is invented as a cure for heartburn. Clove gum, invented at the same time, got its sales boost by being handed out in illegal liquor houses during Prohibition as a breath freshener.

1880 - The popular Halloween candy, candy corn, was invented. Nearly 9 billion candy corn are produced a year.

1877 - Turkish Delight is first recorded as being available for consumption.

1893 - Good & Plenty is the oldest candy made in the United States.

1876 - Milton Snavely Hershey founds Hershey's.

1896
• Cracker Jack is invented by two brothers who sold the recipe at the first Chicago World's Fair. When the first customer tasted the peanut, popcorn, and molasses, he screamed, "That's crackerjack!" which was slang for really good.

• Leo Hirschfield creates the Tootsie Roll, naming it after his daughter's nickname, Tootsie. This was the first candy individually wrapped for freshness.

1870 - Thomas Adam's produces Black Jack, the first manufactured gum.

1866 - NECCO begins to manufacture Conversation Hearts in factories. Since the 20th century, more than 250 billion hearts have been produced.

1847 - NECCO Wafers, a multi-colored, fat-free wafer available in eight flavors, begins production.

1760 - Baker's Chocolate created "La Belle Chocolatiere." Their image of a chocolate-beverage-serving lady has graced the BAKER'S Chocolate package for more than 122 years, making her the oldest product trademark in America.

1502 - Christopher Columbus brings the cocoa bean to Spain.

1800 - "Penny Candy" begins, in which drug-stores sold confections out of large glass jars.

1824 - John Cadbury starts roasting and grinding chocolate beans to flavor his tea. Shortly thereafter, Cadbury Chocolate Company in England invents the first chocolate bar.

1813 - Ice cream is introduced by Quaker colonists and is served at President James Madison's inaugural ball.

[...] Mayans [...]le found from [...]ra Evergreen [...]ch is a natural [chewing] gum. [mat]erial was used by [...]many years later.

CANDY URBAN LEGENDS

We've all heard these myths about sweets and wondered, "Could it be true?" Debunking the biggest candy myths . . .

★ *Mikey from the Life cereal commercial died eating Pop Rocks with soda.* More likely, this was a tall tale invented by nervous moms. The powerful explosions of Pop Rocks set off by carbonated soda still were not strong enough to erupt Mikey's digestive system. Pop Rocks wouldn't still be legal.

★ *Green M&M's are aphrodisiacs.* Whatever turns you on! But there's no ingredient in this color that's any different from the rest. However, people *do* think they can taste the different-colored shells.

★ *Swallowed gum stays in the human stomach for seven years.* Unlike most candy, gum doesn't dissolve fast. That's because gum base, which allows gum to be so chewy, is designed to resist the enzymes in saliva that break down food. But even enzymes and acid will break down the gum, recognize it as waste, and pass it through our digestive system in 24 to 72 hours.

★ *Bubble Yum is chewy owing to spiders' eggs and legs inside it. Kids woke up with spiderwebs covering their face when they chewed it.* This rumor arose from speculation around how much chewier and easier it was to quickly blow a bubble with Bubble Yum, compared to gums invented before it. But the spider story just ain't so!

★ *Candy Canes are a Christian symbol and their J shape is to represent Jesus Christ's first initial.* Nope. A choirmaster in seventeenth-century Germany made them in the shape of a shepherd's crook and passed them out to kids during the Christmas celebration.

CELEBRITIES AT DYLAN'S CANDY BAR

Some of the world's most influential people have come into Dylan's Candy Bar. No matter how successful or famous they are, they immediately become a kid again around the candy. We've designed a section in the store called Famous Favorites, where celebrities' favorite candies are featured inside a Dylan's Candy Bar mini bin that they autograph. Here's what they scoop up.

★ **Alex Rodriguez** (Yankee third baseman): SweetTarts and Dylan's Candy Bar Oreo Cheesecake ice cream

★ **Ashley Olsen** (actress/designer): Sour Gummy Worms

★ **Beyoncé** (performer): Sugar-free red gummy candy

★ **Bill Clinton** (former U.S. president): PayDay

★ **Martha Stewart** (author and TV host): Bazooka

★ **Mary Kate Olsen** (actress/designer): Tootsie Roll

★ **Janet Jackson** (performer): caramels and caramel apples

★ **Jerry Seinfeld** (comedian): Bit-O-Honey

★ **Jon Bon Jovi** (performer): Bubble Tape (for his kids)

★ **Oprah** (talk show host): Fruit slices and nostalgic candies

★ **Madonna** (performer): Red Hots

★ **P. Diddy** (performer): SweetTarts Shockers

★ **Ralph Lauren** (designer): Buttercrunch

★ **Steven Spielberg** (director): Jelly beans and Hot Tamales

BRAIN CANDY
COMMANDER-IN-CHIEF CONFECTIONS

★ In 1813, ice cream (which was introduced in the United States by Quaker colonists) was served at **President James Madison's** inaugural ball.

★ Contrary to popular belief, the Baby Ruth candy bar was not named after the great baseball player Babe Ruth. The Curtiss Candy Company maintains that the confection (made of chocolate-covered peanuts, caramel, and nougat) was named Baby Ruth after President Grover Cleveland's eldest daughter, Ruth, who died of diphtheria.

★ **President Ronald Reagan's** love for jelly beans is historic. He started eating them when he gave up smoking in the early 1960s. On his first day as governor of California, candymaker and CEO of Jelly Belly Herm Rowland presented Reagan with a large jar of jelly beans, which the president liked to keep in his Cabinet Room

Look closely: mosaics are made out of Jelly Belly jelly beans.

for important White House meetings (and he kept a stash of Jelly Belly's on Air Force One). Reagan also suggested to his department chiefs that they eat Jelly Belly's when they needed an energy boost. More than 40 million jelly beans were eaten at Reagan's 1980 inaugural balls. He even launched them into space in 1983, when he ordered that they be stowed as a presidential surprise for the astronauts on the space shuttle *Challenger*. In 1984, Jelly Belly actually invented a blueberry bean, so that Reagan could munch on red, white, and blue.

★ Even the most powerful men have a soft spot for their favorite sweet: **President Bill Clinton,** PayDay; **President George W. Bush,** M&M's and Texas Trash; **President Barack Obama,** salted caramels.

CANDY QUIZ
CANDY IN POP CULTURE!

From Lucy (Lucille Ball) stuffing her face with chocolates to *High School Musical*'s Troy and Gabriella sharing a sweet picnic, candy has always played a big role on TV and in movies—and in books, too. How closely were you paying attention to these sweet scenes? Take this quiz, then rate yourself below:

1. On *Seinfeld*, which candy accidentally lands in a patient's body during surgery (thanks to Kramer)?

   (a) Pez
   (b) Junior Mints
   (c) Bazooka Gum

2. In the movie *Caddyshack,* this candy bar fell into the country club pool and was confused with "doody."

   (a) Baby Ruth
   (b) Charleston Chew
   (c) Twix

3. In *High School Musical 3,* Troy and Gabriella picnic with which treat?

   (a) Red and white jelly beans
   (b) Crème brûlée
   (c) Chocolate-covered strawberries

4. This candy was *not* in the Roald Dahl book *Charlie and the Chocolate Factory.*

   (a) cavity-filling caramels
   (b) chocolate-covered slugs
   (c) Luminous Lollies

5. In *Twilight,* Jacob and Bella share which sweet at La Push beach?

   (a) Gummy spiders
   (b) Twizzlers
   (c) Junior Mints

6. In *The Wizard of Oz*, Dorothy is greeted by which group?

   (a) The Lollipop Guild
   (b) The Popcorn Union
   (c) The Butterscotch Boys of America

7. Which is *not* a character on the Candy Land game board?

   (a) Mr. Grapehead
   (b) Mr. Mint
   (c) Grandma Nutt

8. In *Harry Potter,* the name of the candy store in the town of Hogsmeade is:

   (a) Hogs and Heffers
   (b) Bertie Botts
   (c) Honey Dukes

9. The following character was sent out of Willy Wonka's factory first:

   (a) Veruca Salt
   (b) Violet Beauregarde
   (c) Augustus Gluup

10. In *I Love Lucy*, which is Lucy and Ethel's job on the candy factory assembly line?

   (a) to box the chocolates
   (b) to wrap the chocolates
   (c) to taste the chocolates

11. In *Home Alone*, which candy does Santa offer and say, "Don't spoil your supper!"?

   (a) Nerds
   (b) Tic Tacs
   (c) Buttercrunch

12. In *Beetlejuice*, which candy bar does Beetlejuice hold as he emerges from the Astroturf?

   (a) Zagnut
   (b) Wonka
   (c) Peanut brittle

13. In *Honey, I Blew Up the Kids*, which candy is gigantic and thrown by a baby on a NYC taxicab?

   (a) Starlight mint
   (b) Pez
   (c) Sour ball

14. Which candy does Susan Sarandon eat in her convertible in *Thelma and Louise*?

   (a) Licorice
   (b) Peanut Chews
   (c) Candy corn

15. Which cartoon character loves Butterfingers?

   (a) Fred Flintstone
   (b) Pokémon
   (c) Bart/Homer Simpson

ANSWERS:
1. b, 2. a, 3. c, 4. b, 5. b, 6. a, 7. a, 8. c,
9. c, 10. b, 11. b, 12. a, 13. a, 14. a, 15. c.

....

If you got 10–15 answers correct: So it was you who we heard singing "Pour Some Sugar on Me" in the shower! You eat, sleep, and breathe sugar. A knowledge like yours deserves to be rewarded: treat yourself today to a double helping of your favorite candy (and don't share!).

If you got 6–10 answers correct: Either you're a pretty good guesser or you know a thing or two about the candy biz. So here's one more bonus question to up your score: How many M&M's of each color are in a jumbo bag? Better start counting . . . and eating! And by the way, if you want to know, it's usually 30 percent brown; 20 percent each yellow and red; 10 percent each orange, green, and blue!

If you got fewer than 5 answers correct: You're sorely in need of a candy crash course, and quick! Sample the treat mentioned in each question then try again. If you still strike out, at least you'll have a sugar rush!

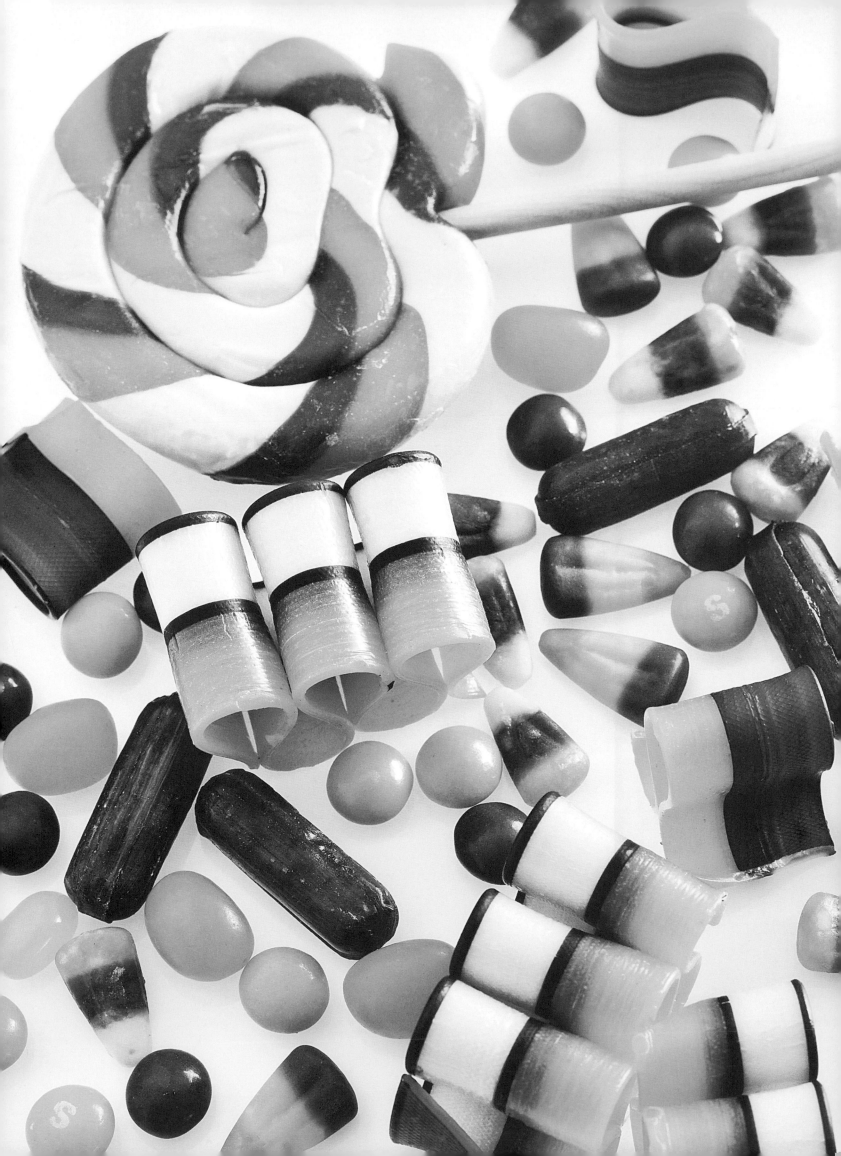

HALLOWEEN

FRIGHT NIGHT

You're never too old for Halloween. If the last time you actually dressed up in costume and went trick-or-treating was the fifth grade, I have news for you: you're seriously missing out on some grown-up good times. Halloween is the one night you can ditch your everyday persona and become someone totally new, different, exciting, even shocking. Let loose; release your inhibitions! Don that naughty nurse costume or fly around like Superman. Halloween grants you a free pass to live out your fantasies.

Halloween can also be the ultimate singles event. Meet and greet while you trick-or-treat! What better way to flirt with a crush than when you're hidden behind a disguise and have candy to offer as an ice breaker?

If you don't feel like going out, stay in and throw your own fright night. Dim the lights, turn on some mood music, and curl up with a scary novel by Edgar Allan Poe or Stephen King, or read *Twilight*—and enjoy a bowl of your favorite Halloween candy (so you'll nibble that, not your nails!). Or invite over some friends for a marathon of great horror movies and whip up some wicked cocktails or bloody candied and caramel apples. Offer your hot neighbor some candy and an apple à la Eve. He won't be able to resist your tricks—or the treat.

BRAIN CANDY
A BRIEF BOO-OGRAPHY OF HALLOWEEN

Halloween dates back two thousand years ago to Ireland and the ancient Celtic festival of Samhain (*saw-in*). The Celts believed that the night before the new year (for them, November 1), the worlds of the living and dead became magically merged.

BRAIN CANDY
HALLOWEEN FUN FACTS

- On average, Americans spend $44 on Halloween candy annually.
- Approximately $2 billion is spent on Halloween candy each year in the United States. People buy more candy during this holiday than on any other—including Christmas, Easter, and Valentine's Day!
- Almost every child under the age of twelve goes trick-or-treating—93 percent of kids—every year.
- About 50 percent of adults dress up for Halloween.
- Approximately 10 percent of pets are dressed in Halloween costumes by their owners.

CANDY ICON
THE JACK O' LANTERN

The old legend of "Stingy Jack" tells of a man who invites the Devil to have a drink with him, and the Devil is tricked by him into paying the bar bill. When Jack dies, God won't let him into heaven, and the Devil won't let him into hell. So Jack has no other choice but to wander the night with a burning coal housed in a carved-out turnip to light his path. The Irish named the ghostly figure "Jack of the Lantern" and many of the early jack-o'-lanterns were frightful faces carved into turnips and potatoes—not pumpkins—to scare off Jack and other evil spirits.

CANDY ICON
CANDY CORN

In 1880, candy corn was invented by the Wonderle Candy Company. In 1898, the Goelitz Confectionery Company began commercial production of these sugary spikes in Cincinnati. The candy was a favorite among farmers because it looked like the crops they grew. More than 35 million pounds of candy corn will be produced each year. And it isn't just for Halloween. There's also reindeer corn for Christmas (red, green, and white); Indian corn for Thanksgiving (brown, yellow, and white); cupid corn for Valentine's Day (red, pink, and white); and bunny corn for Easter (pastel colored). There's even cherry, tangerine, s'mores, and green apple candy corns!

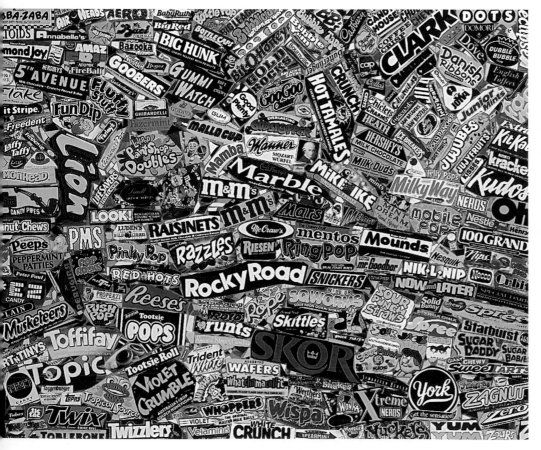

BRAIN CANDY
TRICK-OR-TREATING

The British can take credit for the first trick-or-treating. The tradition was originally part of the All Soul's Day celebration on November 2. Poor people would knock on doors begging for food and would be given "soul cakes" by the housewives in residence. This practice became known as "going a souling," and the beggers, called "soulers," would pray for the dead in exchange for the food. Later, the town's children—both the rich and the poor ones—would go door-to-door "begging" for apples, buns, and money.

TREAT YOURSELF/TRICK OTHERS
HOW TO GET TWICE AS MUCH CANDY ON HALLOWEEN

No matter what age you are, Halloween is a day when diets and portion control can and should go out the window. After all, you aren't supposed to be your *normal* self on this day.

- Always wear a costume that is creative. People will want to reward you for the effort you put in.

- Don't dress too scarily or scantily (you'll scare people away!) Funny, cute, and clever is the way to win them over.

- Bring along a cute kid or even a baby (since they can't eat candy, anyway) as "arm candy." You'll be rewarded with extra loot for seeming charitable for taking them trick-or-treating.

- Bring several changes of masks so you can swap into them if you hit a candy gold mine. You can go back for seconds, and they'll never recognize you!

- Start trick-or-treating earlier rather than later, so the good candy doesn't run out or get taken by all the young kids.

- Map out the neighborhoods that are wealthy and have tall buildings.

- Wear comfortable shoes no matter what your costume is, so you can move fast and stand on your feet ringing doorbells for long hours.

- Find a candy drop-off point where you can lighten your load or swap trick-or-treat bags (just in case yours becomes so full that it starts to rip).

- Have a car or be near taxis so you don't have to forfeit any heavy loads.

- Avoid haunted houses or Halloween parties if your mission is to load up on treats. Chances are the variety of candy will be more limited there than at the dozens of homes you collect candy from.

HALLOWEEN IDENTITY CRISIS

If the pressure to pick a Halloween costume is haunting you, try these great candy-themed costumes. While their names may conjure up something innocent, they fall into the "sexy nurse" category. (Check out adult Halloween costumes on Shopzilla.com or Rickysnyc.com.)

- Ms. Candy Apple with worm puppet
- Candy Corn Witch
- Sugar Baby
- Candy Cane Cutie
- Candy Factory Worker
- Candy Striper
- Miss Candy Cane

- Mr. Peppermint
- Candy Girl
- Sugar Daddy
- M&M
- Pez
- Tootsie Roll
- Blow Pop
- Willy Wonka
- Oompa Loompa

THE BEST/WORST HALLOWEEN CANDIES TO GIVE OUT
HAND THESE OUT AND YOU'LL DISAPPOINT TRUE CANDY LOVERS!

- *Apples:* No one wants fruit, unless it's coated in chocolate or caramel.

- *Boxes of raisins:* Ditto. And many trick-or-treaters are over five years old!

- *Granola bars:* You can't fool a candy bar lover with this!

- *Miniature boxes of cereal:* This isn't candy no matter how much sugar it has in it.

- *Baked goods:* They only crumble in the trick-or-treat bag and make a mess.

- *Bags of unpopped microwave popcorn:* People want sweet instant gratification.

- *Canned food:* Trick-or-treaters are not a charity.

- *Carob:* Healthy, yes, but people want the real deal!

- *Tic Tacs:* Small and boring!

- *Stale candy:* It looks as if it has been sitting around since Easter.

- *Sugar-free and hard candies:* Most senior citizens are not trick-or-treating!

- *Pennies, toothbrushes, stickers:* It's a nice thought, but if people can't eat something sweet on the spot, they won't be happy.

THE BEST CANDIES TO GIVE OUT ARE THE BIGGEST OR LAST THE LONGEST—OR EVEN BETTER, COMBINE TWO TREATS IN ONE!

- *King-size candy bars:* Forget the minis promoted in the supermarket.

- *Blow Pops:* You get two-for-one deals: gum and a lollipop!

- *Lollipop Paint Shop:* Colorful sugar and a lollipop that looks like a paintbrush. You can even paint the sugar on your tongue!

- *Pop Rocks:* These are entertaining candies. They take a while to eat unless you are daring and like it loud!

- *Atomic Fireballs:* If you can stand it, they last a long time.

- *Candy Buttons:* It takes a while to bite them all off the paper.

- *Astronaut Ice Cream:* It lasts three years compared to normal ice cream.

- *Razzles:* Tart candy that turns into gum!

ENTERTAINING WITH CANDY
CREEPY CANDY

Halloween is one of my favorite holidays to entertain. There are so many truly disgusting candies that add shock value and fun. I'm particularly fond of serving Hotlix, which are lollipops that have real cockroaches, crickets, and worms in them. I like to skewer gummy insects like spiders, flies, and larvae and offer them for dipping in a cauldron of mud (chocolate sauce). I pass around a platter of "blood and guts": candy body parts such as crunchy fingers, toes, gooey brains, and gummy or chocolate eyeballs with a lab beaker of cherry Jell-O (blood) and lime Jell-O (guts). I also like to surprise guests with strategically placed gummy rats, snakes, and tarantulas. These gummy creatures are so realistic in the way they look and feel that biting into them is even more frightening! And one of the most wicked treats is Jelly Belly Bean Boozled beans. They may look normal, but they taste vile, in flavors ranging from boogers and ear wax to vomit and skunk spray!

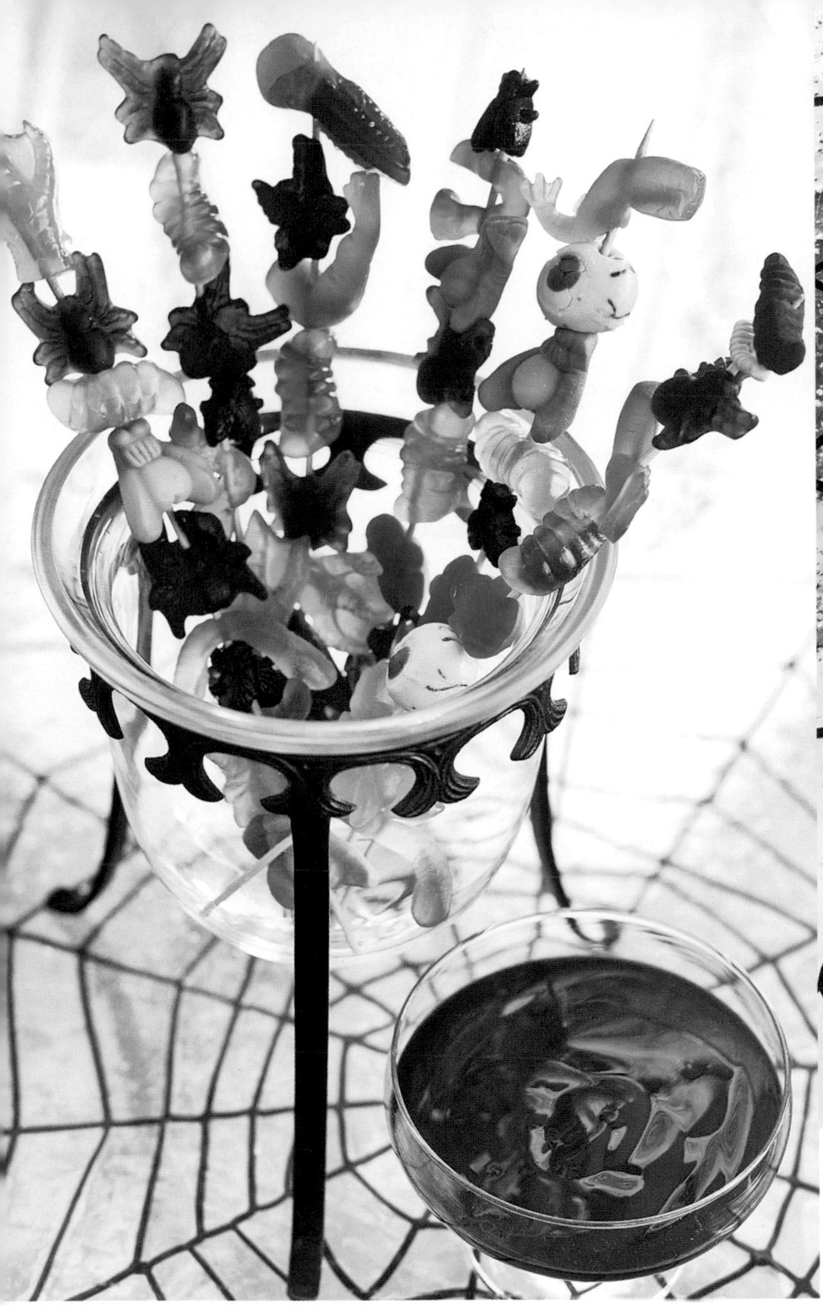

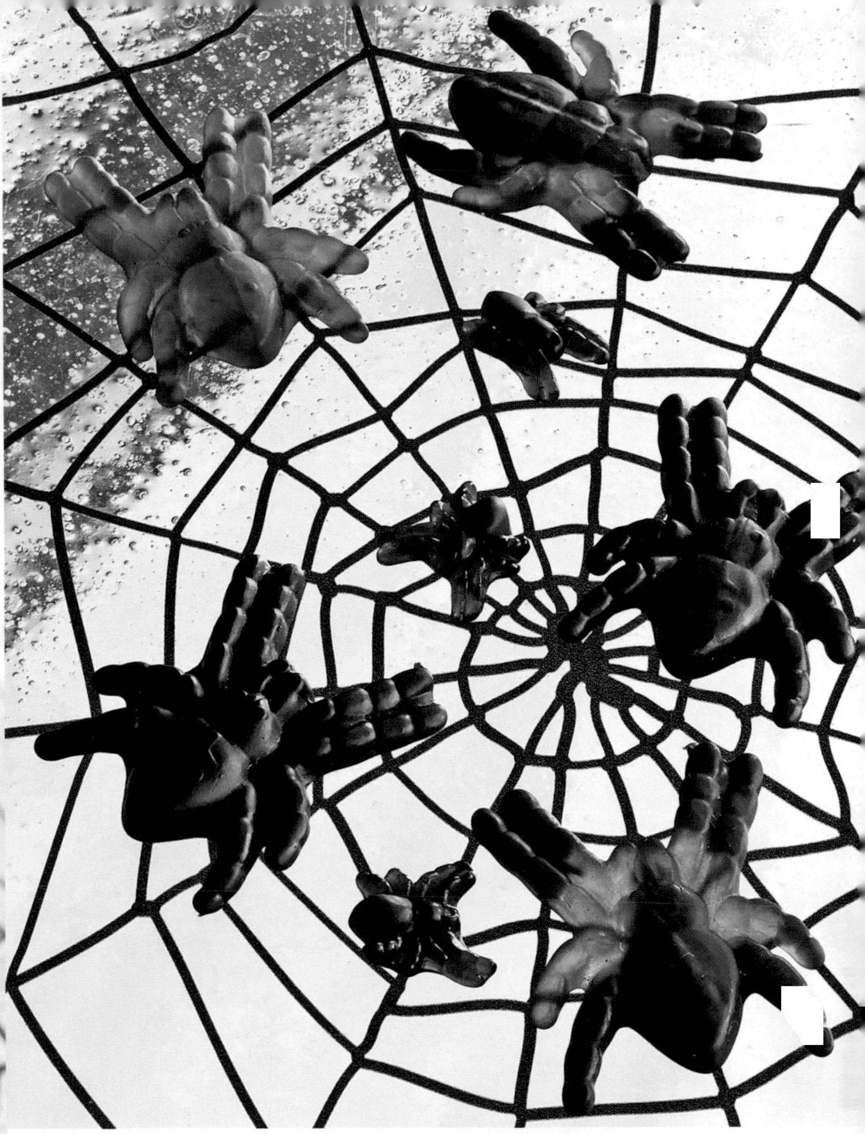

DYLAN'S CANDY BAR
BLACK WIDOW

1 serving

1½ ounces (3 tablespoons) vanilla vodka

½ ounce (1 tablespoon) black anise-flavored liqueur

1 tablespoon espresso

Ice cubes

Garnish: black licorice wheels and gummy spiders

Glassware: martini glass

In a cocktail shaker, combine the vodka, liqueur, and espresso with ice cubes. Shake to mix and put in a glass. Unwind the black licorice wheels slightly and attach them and the spiders to the rim of the glass.

WARNING!
NOT COOL IF YOU'RE NOT 21

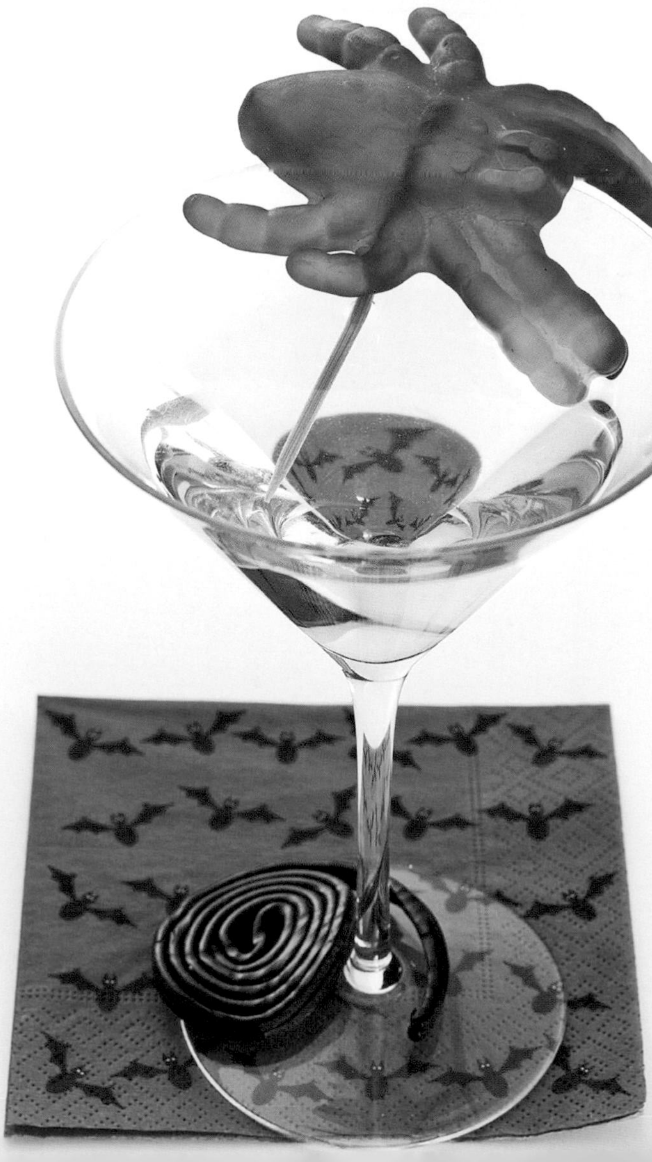

DYLAN'S CANDY BAR
VAMPIRE COSMO

1 serving

2 tablespoons fresh lime juice (about 2 limes)
Red sugar ("Pucker Powder") or a cherry Pixy Stix
1½ ounces (3 tablespoons) vodka
¾ ounce (1½ tablespoons) triple sec
¾ ounce (1½ tablespoons) cranberry juice
Ice cubes
Glassware: cosmopolitan glass
Garnish: wax fangs

Dip the rim of a cosmo glass into the lime juice and then dip again into the cherry-flavored colored sugar. Pour the vodka, triple sec, cranberry juice, and lime juice into a cocktail shaker with ice. Shake well. Strain into the glass and attach the wax fang to the rim.

WARNING!
NOT COOL IF YOU'RE NOT 21 ↑

DYLAN'S CANDY BAR
CARAMEL APPLES

Makes 6 caramel apples

6 small tart apples, such as Granny Smith
6 (4- to 5-inch) popsicle sticks
Vegetable oil spray
½ cup each assorted candy toppings (mini chocolate chips, sprinkles, candy corn, mini marshmallows)
1 (14 ounce) bag soft caramels, unwrapped
2 tablespoons rum, coffee liqueur, coffee, or water

Wash the apples and pat them dry. Remove any stems and insert a popsicle stick where the stem was, about 1 inch into the center. Line a baking sheet with aluminum foil and lightly spray it with vegetable oil. Have the toppings ready in separate bowls.

Combine the caramels and rum in a small, heavy saucepan. Melt over moderate heat, stirring constantly with a wooden spoon until smooth and combined well. Immediately, working with one apple at a time, and tilting the saucepan and apple, dip each apple, turning it to coat three-fourths of it and leaving the stem end exposed. Let excess caramel drip back into the pan—take time to do this or your toppings will not adhere and you won't have enough caramel mixture for remaining apples. Immediately dip the apple in the desired topping on bottom and halfway up sides. Transfer apples as dipped to prepared sheet pan. Let apples stand at cool room temperature or chill until caramel is set and firm. Serve on a platter.

THANKSGIVING

BE THANKFUL

When you're invited for Thanksgiving, or even to a home-cooked meal at someone's home, the most polite thing to do is to bring a gift. A candy gift is perfectly thoughtful and special. It says "I appreciate you—and I'm the kind of guest you want to have back again . . . and again."

For the lady who lunches, I suggest petit fours and decorative tins of Parisian pastilles to freshen her breath. They can even accessorize her handbag. For the Martha Stewart wannabe, there are chocolate flowers planted in green jelly beans in a handpainted pot, and gardening gloves. Avid golfers won't get "teed off" if you give them white chocolate golf balls, while "the ticket" for a movie buff includes gourmet caramel-covered popcorn, boxes of concession candy, and a collection of his or her favorite DVDs. A musician might enjoy a CD mix of candy songs paired with Hershey's Symphony Bars and Mozart Chocolate Truffles. And a Wall Street broker would love to count on some money-themed sweets: 100 Grand bars, Barton's Million Dollar Bars, and chocolate-foiled coins. Last but not least, for the baseball fan, fill a mitt with a Big League Chew, a Baby Ruth, baseball cards, Pop Shot's candy-filled baseballs, and a Pez dispenser of his or her favorite team. Score!

If you don't really know the person who's hosting very well, never fear: simply tuck a gift certificate to his or her favorite restaurant or store inside the wrapper of a chocolate bar and say it's a treat for preparing such a lovely meal!

DECORATING WITH CANDY
SUGAR-COAT THE TABLE

By all means, break out the good china and linens and polish the silver. Thanksgiving is all about the festive feast, so you should showcase the food in your prettiest plates and platters. I recommend embellishing the table with candy for a more memorable display: a foiled chocolate turkey at each place setting; instead of flowers, try maple-leaf–shaped sugar cookies or a vase brimming with glorious fall foliage (they're really chocolate leaves); and a candy cornucopia filled with marzipan vegetables that spill out across the length of the table, tempting guests to dig in, and not even wait for dessert.

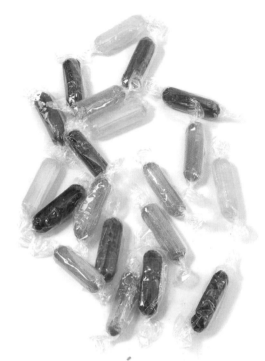

BRAIN CANDY
THANKSGIVING

Most people regard the Plymouth colonists' and Wampanoag Indians' autumn harvest feast in 1621 as the first Thanksgiving. The meal was a symbol of the cooperation between the English colonists and the Native Americans.

CANDY ICON
THE CORNUCOPIA

The traditional cornucopia is a curved goat's horn brimming with fruits and grains. It is called the horn of plenty. According to Greek legend, Amalthea (a goat) broke one of her horns and offered it to the Greek god Zeus in reverence. As a thank-you, Zeus later set the goat's image in the sky as the constellation Capricorn. Today, we use a cone-shaped wicker basket and fill it with a variety of treats in autumnal colors.

CANDY CRAFT
CANDY CORNUCOPIA

MATERIALS

Horn-shaped basket

Tissue paper in orange, brown, tan, green

Ribbon

Masking tape

Vegetable-shaped marzipan

Scissors

Paper leaves (optional)

Step 1. Stuff the basket with tissue paper and fan out the variety of colors at the opening of the basket.

Step 2. Tie a ribbon around the edge of the basket's opening (to make the centerpiece seem like a "present" to guests).

Step 3. Cut 1-inch squares of masking tape. Fold them and place tape under each marzipan piece.

Step 4. Fill the cornucopia with marzipan, starting at the back of the basket.

Step 5. Accessorize by scattering leaves around the marzipan.

CANDY ICON
THE TURKEY

The menu at the first Thanksgiving feast was thought to include wild fowl, such as turkey. The turkey later became a symbol of the holiday, mainly because it is native to North America and also because it's a big bird that serves a lot of people.

CANDY CRAFT
TURKEY PILGRIM HAT

MATERIALS

1 paper pilgrim hat

2 paperweights (or a 1-pound object of any sort)

Glue gun and glue sticks

Scissors

Turkey-themed candies:

4 lollipops

3 candy canes

About 6 decorated gumballs

Step 1. Set the hat on a table and put the paperweights on the left and right sides of the brim.

Step 2. Plug in the glue gun.

Step 3. Apply a drop of glue to four places on the front rim and two places on the top of the hat. Adhere the decorated gumballs.

Step 4. Stick the pointed end of the scissors into the left and right sides of the hat and two areas on the top of the hat. Slide in the lollipops.

Step 5. Stick the pointed end of the scissors into three places on the top of the hat. Twist the scissors in each place to create a hole where a candy stick can fit. Slide in the candy canes.

Step 6. Glue a fourth candy climber onto the side of the hat by adhering glue where the top and bottom of the candy cane meet the hat. Hold the candy cane onto the glue for 5 seconds.

Step 7. You can wear the hat at the Thanksgiving meal or use it as a centerpiece.

THE URGE TO SPLURGE

Most people I know do not come even close to consuming the amount of candy that I do on Thanksgiving or any day. They cannot handle more than a few bites of something sweet without complaining of a headache or nausea. I, however, have an incredible knack for being able to eat an unlimited amount of sweets without feeling sick. Fortunately, my favorite candies these days (marshmallows, red Swedish Fish, and gumballs) are fat-free. Otherwise, I'd be in a lot of trouble with my trainer!

However, sometimes after a stressful day, or even to kick off a month of healthy eating, I'll treat myself to whatever I'm craving and seriously indulge (so much for the monotonous salads of mixed greens and vegetables!). Dinner will become a heaping bowl of cake-batter ice cream, in which I mix mountains of Marshmallow Fluff and yellow cake. Then, for dessert (since the ice cream was just the first course, of course), I prefer the vanilla icing off a black-and-white cookie, marshmallow divinity, or a Rice Krispie Treat.

Some people shy away from candy because they think sugar is the enemy. Unless you are following strict doctor's orders, that's tragic! You don't know what you're missing (or maybe you do, and that's even sadder!). I don't subscribe to complete deprivation. I think that is actually bad for the body, and I know it's not healthy for the soul. The more you tell yourself, "I can't have it," the more you'll want it. That leads to feeling lousy, not to mention guilty when you finally give in to your craving (and trust me, you will).

You don't have to banish all treats from your diet. Everything in moderation (except on splurge days). In fact, many dietitians profess that a little of what you crave is perfectly okay. Rule of thumb: 100 calories makes for a sensible snack. It may sound insignificant, but it actually translates into an abundance of sweet treats. As long as you are not eating Chunky bars or mounds of Mounds on a daily basis, having your favorite treat once in a while will not do you any harm. In fact, I guarantee it will make you a happier, better-adjusted human being. If you bite into a candy bar, you're less likely to bite a nasty person's head off. So go on—treat yourself!

WORK IT! OWN IT!

My trainer, Tony, knows that taste-testing candy all day is my job. So he's great at helping me stay fit—and burn more than 100 calories fast. There's the traditional exercise approach: jump rope for 10 minutes; bike for 8 to 9 minutes at 90 rpm; run a mile; play tennis for 30 minutes. And then there's a more creative way: slow-dance to seven songs; give someone you love a 20-minute massage; watch 90 minutes of *Seinfeld* episodes (laughing also works your abs!); vacuum or push a baby stroller for a half hour. Even more fun, unwrap a chocolate bar (you just burned .5 calories) or chew gum all day (you'll burn 10 calories per minute). Drink ice water after your bag of jelly beans. Experts say you'll expend about 123 calories of heat to warm the water to body temperature. There are endless ways to work off your treats and plenty that don't involve setting foot in a gym. So you can literally have your cake and eat it, too!

WHY WEIGHT?
100-CALORIE SWEETS

- 5 chocolate graham crackers
- 4 Hershey's Kisses
- 1 snack size ("fun size") candy bar
- 3 Twizzlers
- 3 medium Peeps
- 10 large jelly beans
- 16 pieces candy corn
- 2/3 cup mini marshmallows
- 4.5 Tootsie Roll Midgets
- 3 Laffy Taffy squares

STUFFED!

At Thanksgiving, most Americans give themselves permission to devour practically everything on the table, despite what their stomachs and consciences tell them. I think eating like this is okay every now and then, as long as you get back on track and eat healthfully. If you want to feel better about yourself, incorporate more vegetables and fruits into your diet. Sugar can actually help "make the medicine go down" if you pair these "good for you" foods with sweet condiments: honey + grapefruit; caramel + apple; chocolate + fruit; peanut butter + celery; marshmallow + yam; brown sugar + squash; cinnamon + glazed carrots; molasses + baked beans; candied walnuts + spinach; chocolate + fruit (after all chocolate is a vegetable—it comes from a bean!).

COOKING WITH CANDY

SEA BASS CRUSTED WITH SESAME SEED CANDIES

Sea bass encrusted with sesame seed candies was one of the fan-favorite dishes created by Chef Robert Irvine on Food Network's *Dinner Impossible:* when he was challenged to make a feast incorporating candy at Dylan's Candy Bar. I think it would make for a yummy main course at Thanksgiving—or any other day!

Serves 6 (appetizer portion)

16 Joyva sesame seed candies
1 cup panko bread crumbs
3 teaspoons chopped fresh tarragon leaves
2 teaspoons chopped fresh chives
3 tablespoons canola oil, plus 4 tablespoons for cooking fish
2 pounds fresh sea bass, cut into 6 portions
2 teaspoons stone-ground mustard
Salt and freshly ground black pepper

Grind the sesame seed candies into a rough powder, leaving a few chunks for texture.

Preheat the oven to 350°F.

Mix the bread crumbs, herbs, ground sesame seed candies, and the 3 tablespoons oil in a small bowl. The oil should wet the crumbs and will help to keep the crumbs on the fish.

In a large, hot skillet, heat the 4 tablespoons canola oil. When the oil is hot, add the fish and sear one side until golden brown. Remove the fish from the pan to a large ovenproof serving dish and allow to cool slightly, around 3 minutes.

Using a spatula, flip the fish over and lightly coat the seared side of the fish with the mustard. Cover the top of the fish with the bread crumb mixture. Bake in the preheated oven until flesh is firm, about 12 minutes. Serve immediately.

HANUKKAH & CHRISTMAS

CANDY CURE-ALLS

During the hustle and bustle of the holiday season, when you're stressed to find the perfect gift for everyone, is when you're most likely to come down with some illness. It's freezing, and contagious colds and the flu are inescapable, especially in crowded stores.

As soon as December rolls around, I stock up on more candy than ever. It has become my saving grace to help me endure the cold months ahead. Just seeing the bright colors of candy or the shimmering foiled packaging immediately brightens my day.

Candy can also help you recover from a host of winter illnesses. Chewing gum like Bazooka and Dubble Bubble helps relieve my sinuses and earaches. I always make sure to pack gum on a trip, particularly when I'm congested. I pop it in 30 minutes before the plane's descent, and it helps relieve the pressure on my ear drums. The action of chewing gum opens up the eustachian tubes.

According to the Wrigley Science Institute and the American Dietetic Association, chewing gum is actually good for your health and figure. Most people know that chewing sugar-free gum can help prevent cavities and freshen breath. But now, the institute's research says it may be a tool "to help manage weight, increase focus, alertness and concentration, and help relieve life's everyday stresses." Coaches often advise athletes to chomp away so they keep their heads in the game; and psychologists theorize that it can help people release nervous energy and provide an outlet for frustration and irritation. Don't get mad, get chewing!

When I have a sore throat, I soothe it by sucking on candies like Jolly Ranchers and Nestlé's Werther Original Hard Candies. Mint candies, especially Altoids and candy canes, cool and relieve my respiratory system. And I've found lollipops useful if I'm confined to bed; you can suck on them while lying down and not have to worry about choking! They're also a comfort candy and bring back my childhood memories of getting a lolly from the pediatrician's office.

Honey is another sweet and ancient remedy for sore throats. I definitely prefer it to cough medicine! If you put a few drops of honey and Lemonheads into hot water and sip, it helps loosen phlegm. Honey is also a great topical solution for dressing wounds and healing burns.

If someone has the flu, I've often prescribed cinnamon candies like Red Hots and Hot Tamales. They actually can increase the temperature on your tongue and alleviate the chills. Plus, the spicy taste is enlivening.

And for centuries, black licorice has provided relief from constipation and mint candies have been used to soothe the effects of stomach flu.

Chocolate is magical for beating the blizzard blues. It gives you the needed serotonin and magnesium boost you can't get easily in the darkness of winter. A cup of hot cocoa is the perfect winter remedy—better than chicken noodle soup!

GET CREATIVE WITH YOUR COCOA!

- Instead of traditional marsh-mallows, add a Snowman Peep to your cup of cocoa for a cute and creamy topper.

- Make your own version of Aztec hot chocolate by adding ¼ teaspoon chili powder, ¼ teaspoon nutmeg, and ½ teaspoon cinnamon to milk before steaming.

- For a minty twist, stir your cocoa with a candy cane or add a few fresh mint leaves to the hot milk and let it soak for 8 to 10 minutes. Dunk in a Peppermint Patty!

- Brew a white hot chocolate: use 2 ounces finely chopped white chocolate instead of dark chocolate and no sugar.

- Make a chai cocoa by changing the above white hot chocolate: heat milk with 1 small cinnamon stick, ¼ teaspoon ground cardamon, 2 whole cloves, and ¼ teaspoon black peppercorns. Whisk in the white chocolate until smooth, pour the mixture through a sieve, and discard the spices. Best served with gingerbread cookies!

- Want a cocoa with a kick? For those twenty-one years old and above, stir in an ounce of Kahlua, Irish cream, hazelnut liqueur, or peppermint schnapps. Drop in rum cordials.

COOKING WITH CANDY

DYLAN'S CANDY BAR HOT CHOCOLATE

Makes 1 cup

1 cup whole milk

5 tablespoons (1½ ounces) Dylan's Candy Bar Belgian Chocolate Shavings or 1½ ounces good-quality dark chocolate or milk chocolate, finely chopped

1 teaspoon sugar (if using dark chocolate)

2 spoonfuls whipped cream

1 tablespoon mini marshmallows

Heat the milk in a small, heavy saucepan just to a simmer over moderately low heat.

Whisk in the chocolate and, if needed, the sugar. Whisk until chocolate is melted and mixture is smooth. Serve in a mug, topped with whipped cream, marshmallows, and extra chocolate shavings.

BRAIN CANDY
HOT COCOA VS. HOT CHOCOLATE

Oh, the weather outside is frightful . . . but hot cocoa's so delightful! The Aztecs get credit for creating this drink. They used the roasted cocoa bean, but it was served cold, flavored with wine and chiles, and not at all sweet. In the early 1500s, chocolate was discovered and brought back to Europe by the explorer Hernando Cortés. The Spanish, however, made their cocoa hot, sweet (*gracias!*), and without the fiery hot peppers. Eventually, it made its way to American shores, where we made it our own winter wonder—and better!

Hot cocoa and hot chocolate are not the same thing, although people often use the terms interchangeably. Hot cocoa is made from cocoa powder, the result of extracting most of the cocoa butter from the ground cacao beans (so it's lower in fat). Hot chocolate, on the other hand, is made directly from bar chocolate, which already contains cocoa, sugar, and cocoa butter (so it's sweeter and richer).

HOW TO LIVE THE SWEET LIFE WHEN SURVIVING THE WINTER BLUES

Temperatures are dropping below freezing. You've run out of room on your calendar to schedule appointments. Your friends are enjoying socializing on the weekends while you slave away at the office. Your family is giving you a guilt trip. The computer died and your PowerPoint presentation got wiped out. No matter what your personal predicament, one thing is clear: you sure could use a vacation!

But here's the sweet solution. You don't have to hop on a plane, bus, or train to escape the everyday. You could make a home spa. Take a long, hot bubble bath, then exfoliate and moisturize with Dylan Candy Bar's Re-Treat products. Their scents, such as Chocolate Cupcake and Vanilla Birthday Cake Batter, will bring back comforting childhood memories (like a mom baking in the kitchen). Light an aromatic candle scented in caramel or gingerbread. And if you need to feel energized, spritz a sweet and citrusy home fragrance of lemon drop or peppermint. One deep breath and you'll be feeling better. If winter leaves you looking as white as a marshmallow, warm up your complexion with a purple scarf and bubblegum pink lip gloss.

Once you emerge from your "scent-sational" experience, it's time to crank up the holiday music with uplifting candy lyrics: "Marshmallow World in Winter" and "Hard Candy Christmas." Or take a hot shower and rock out (in privacy) to a lollipop tune. Winter won't seem so dull if you sing:

- "Put Your Lollipop Away," Blues Traveler
- "My Boy Lollipop," Spice Girls
- "Lollipop," Mika
- "Lollipop," Lil Wayne
- "On the Good Ship Lollipop," Shirley Temple

And finally, if you can't get a beach vacation tan or can't go abroad just now, why not transport yourself to another culture by learning a new language? That way, when you eventually do take that trip, you will know how to fulfill your sweet tooth anywhere around the globe. See the phrases (above right) to get you started:

chci sladkost je veux des bonbons キャンディーがほしい أريد حلوى quiero dulces ich möchte Süßes voglio delle caramelle אני רוצה סוכריות vreau bomboane gusto kong kendi 난 사탕이 먹고 싶다 我要糖果 eu quero balinha quero doces मुझे टोफ़ी चाहिए я хочу конфетку jag vill ha godis **I WANT CANDY**

HANUKKAH
TRADITION!

Hanukkah, "The Festival of Lights," is celebrated over eight nights, and candy or a homemade candy gift is the perfect thing to give every one of these nights. On Hanukkah, Jewish people light nine candles on the menorah or candelabra (one for each of the successive eight days of the holiday, plus one center candle that lights the others). The menorah symbolizes the candelabra in the ancient Tabernacle and is a link between the past and present.

CANDY ICON
HANUKKAH GELT

Hanukkah is synonymous with *gelt,* which are chocolate coins wrapped in gold and silver foil. The traditional Hanukkah dreidel game involves wagering these candies in place of money, since Jewish law states that you are not to "count your money" by the light of the menorah. Aside from spinning the dreidel, *gelt* can also be hidden around the house for kids to find—a kind of scavenger hunt with a sweet ending!

CANDY CRAFT
CHOCOLATE MENORAH

Instead of real candles, use chocolate ones as a tabletop centerpiece. Invite each guest to take one home as a treat . . . or save them to eat on each night of Hanukkah.

MATERIALS

Glue gun and glue sticks

1 menorah

10 foiled chocolate candles (9 for the menorah and 1 just in case)

Step 1. Heat the glue gun.

Step 2. Dab glue on the base of one candle holder.

Step 3. Wait 5 seconds, until the glue that was just applied cools, so it doesn't cause the chocolate to melt. Then lay the menorah down and hold foiled chocolate candle onto the glue. Press the candle onto the menorah for 5 seconds.

Step 4. Repeat steps 2 and 3 until entire menorah is full.

Step 5. Once the candles seem firmly adhered, set the menorah upright on a special table.

CANDY CRAFT
A WINTER WONDERLAND SLED

If you are not sure of someone's religion, or you're searching for a nondenominational type of gift, this is a beautiful option that makes a great centerpiece for the holiday table—or anywhere else in the house for guests to enjoy.

MATERIALS

Floral Styrofoam

Sled basket

Foiled chocolate star wands, in winter colors, such as white and blue

Marshmallows or paper snow

Hershey's Kisses or any other silver-foil–wrapped candies

Ribbon (silver preferred)

Glue gun (optional)

Cellophane

Chocolate-foiled ornaments (to accessorize the table)

Step 1. Cut Styrofoam to fit the sled.

Step 2. Stick the star wands into the Styrofoam, alternating colors.

Step 3. Cover the Styrofoam with marshmallows or paper snow and Hershey's Kisses.

Step 4. Glue-gun or tie a shiny ribbon around the sled and form a big bow.

Step 5. Wrap the sled in cellophane.

Step 6. Seal the top with a bow and your personal holiday card. Be sure to mention you made this gift yourself!

CHRISTMAS

HOW TO LIVE THE SWEET LIFE . . .
WHEN YOU'RE WORKING FOR SCROOGE

If your boss has a perpetual case of the bah-humbugs, you don't have to be nice, so get naughty with candy!

- Make your own candy dart board (hide it behind the door to your office). Put your boss's picture in the center target, and launch gummy worms and spiders at his or her head whenever you need relief. Childish? Yes, but oh-so-satisfying.

- Send him or her (anonymously, of course) a chocolate sampler box for the holidays—with all the good pieces already eaten.

- Find out what his or her favorite candy is in the vending machine. Then make sure you empty it first thing every day—before those 3 P.M. cravings strike.

- Fill his or her candy dish with real black licorice or sugar-free candies. Both have an intense laxative effect!

- Stick gummy rats in his or her desk drawer—or make it a real "mouse" pad.

- If he or she is on a strict beach-vacation diet, load the candy jar with tempting and irresistible candies and cookies.

CANDY ICON
SANTA CLAUS

The original Santa dates back to the mythological tales of the god Odin, and was influenced by a real fourth-century bishop, Saint Nicholas of Myra, who was famous for his kindness and generosity. The American Santa—complete with his red suit, shiny black boots, white beard, and big belly, came to life in the 1800s, when writer Washington Irving created him, "dropping gifts down the chimneys of his favorites." Dr. Clement Clarke Moore then immortalized Saint Nick in his 1822 poem "The Night Before Christmas."

DECORATING WITH CANDY
DECK THE HALLS

A festive way to bring light into the darkness of winter is to decorate your surroundings with bright colors. Making crafts and decorations using candy is a fun and interactive project to do with friends and family. Whether you have guests coming over or you are bringing someone a holiday gift, these will definitely bring joy to anyone of any age.

- Make a Christmas wreath entirely out of candy. Or save electricity and decorate Christmas wreaths with brightly colored foiled chocolate lights. The shimmering vibrant colors are just as good as the real thing.

- Fill large glass vases with big chocolate ornaments. Eat some for dessert, too!

- Hang foiled chocolate ornaments and holiday-themed lollipops from a Christmas garland or tree.

- Customize Christmas stockings with family members' favorite treats, such as red and green ribbon candy and of course candy canes.

CANDY ORNAMENT–
FILLED VASES

MATERIALS

1 large vase

50 foiled chocolate Christmas ornaments, with
  various decorated foils

Step 1. Fill the vase with assorted Christmas
  ornaments.

Step 2. Place on a ledge, not directly in the sun, or
  on the center of a table.

CANDY CRAFTS
DECORATIVE CANDY WREATH

MATERIALS

Chocolate-foiled ornaments (Christmas balls, bells, poinsettias, lights)

1 real or fake pine wreath

Glue gun

Hook or wire

3-inch-wide red ribbon, 12 inches long

Step 1. Place the chocolate ornaments around the wreath in the position you'd like them.

Step 2. Heat up the glue gun.

Step 3. Place a drop of glue onto the back of a foiled ornament (make sure it isn't too hot so chocolate and foil don't melt). Glue the ornament onto the wreath, holding it in place for 5 seconds.

Step 4. Continue gluing chocolates to the wreath.

Step 5. Tie the wire or hook to the top of the wreath.

Step 6. Tie a bow to the top or bottom of the wreath.

Step 7. Hang and admire!

CANDY TOPIARY

MATERIALS

Glue gun

Hard candy in plastic wrappers (use candy wrapped in red and green Christmas colors or silvery and blue wintery colors; you can use different candies and colors for other holidays as well)

Styrofoam wreath (any size works, but 14-inch is best for displaying on a door or in a window)

1-inch-wide ribbon, about 24 inches long

Step 1. Place a drop of glue on the back of a piece of candy and stick it to the wreath, holding in place for 5 seconds to let it set. Continue gluing candies to the wreath, working from the top to the bottom (in case glue drips down, you can cover it). Cover the wreath until you can barely see the Styrofoam. Overlap the candy to give it a fuller look.

Step 2. Fold the ribbon in half, bringing the ends together. Glue the middle of the ribbon to the top of the wreath, then let it dry.

Step 3. Tie the loose ends of the ribbon together, leaving a loop for hanging.

Step 4. Display and enjoy!

Note: Once the holiday (or party) is over, the candies are edible. Simply cut them off the wreath or slip them out of the plastic wrapper.

CHRISTMAS TREE TOPIARY

MATERIALS

Small block of floral foam

Clay or plastic flower pot (covered with a pretty fabric, ribbon, or stickers, or painted with a design, if you'd like)

2½-foot-long dowel (at a hardware store or craft store)

Spray paint of choice

Pumpkin carver or knife

3-foot-tall Styrofoam cone

Glue gun or Styrofoam glue

Colorful candies in Christmas colors

Ribbon

Step 1. Place the floral foam block in the pot, leaving 1 inch of space at the top.

Step 2. Stick the dowel into the center of the foam inside the pot.

Step 3. Spray-paint the pot and dowel to match the candy theme color.

Step 4. Use the pumpkin carver to cut a hole in the bottom center of the Styrofoam cone to match the width of the dowel so it fits onto dowel snugly. The bottom should be a foot from the top of the dowel.

Step 5. With the glue gun or Styrofoam glue, make horizontal strips of glue from the top of the cone to the bottom. Place the candies next to each other along the strip. Once these candies dry, place the next row of candies under this row.

Step 6. Fill the pot with loose candies to cover the foam and tie a ribbon around the pole.

ENTERTAINING WITH CANDY
CANDIED CHRISTMAS

Foiled-chocolate poinsettias can be bundled into a clear bag and tied with a real poinsettia to help accessorize a present box or guests' napkins at the dining table. The candies also look great inside a centerpiece vase that is topped with a bundle of real poinsettias. Candy cane ornaments are another multipurpose treat. They make for festive napkin rings and seat savers. Guests can also use them to freshen their breath at the Christmas dinner.

CANDY ICON
THE POINSETTIA

Poinsettias are a popular motif for Christmas candy. They are plants native to Mexico. The Mexicans in the eighteenth century thought the plant's yellow starlike center was symbolic of the Star of Bethlehem, and that the red leaves signified the blood of Christ. Therefore, the poinsettia became known as The Christmas Flower. Poinsettias were named after America's first ambassador to Mexico, Joel Poinsett, who brought the plants to America in 1828.

CANDY ICON
GUMDROPS

There are two types of gumdrops: fruit and spice flavored (aka spice drops).

Gumdrops are often used to decorate homes and cookies during Christmastime because they add color and have a snowlike sugar coating. They also compliment flavors such as nutmeg, gingerbread, and cinnamon, which are popular in Christmas baked goods.

CANDY ICON
CANDY CANES

There is much debate about where candy canes come from. Some say it was the fifteenth-century French priests who created a sugar stick in the shape of a shepherd's hooked staff, while others point to a German choirmaster who presented it as a reward to children in church. Some say the candy hooks were used to help hang food and decorations on Christmas trees, while others believe its "J" shape was a metaphor for Jesus Christ. But one thing is known for certain: the first canes were all white and didn't earn their stripes until several years later. In the 1900s, candy manufacturers also decided that the canes needed some "cool" flavorings and gave them a peppermint or wintergreen taste. Now, candy canes of all shapes, sizes, and flavors abound—1.76 billion are made each year. The biggest one in the world measured a towering 58 feet—certainly not fit for stuffing in a stocking!

NEW YEAR'S EVE

SWEET RESOLUTIONS

Anxious about ringing in another year? Not eager to sing "Auld Lang Syne"? Put on those gummy cherry-colored shades because the future is *so* bright! At the eve of every new year, my friends and I share our New Year's resolutions. It's important for closure (the year's over . . . time to move on!) and also for helping yourself mentally make a fresh start and set new plans. I recommend starting the eve by creating a list of long- and short-term goals that are tangible. Then toast to a year of accomplishing all your resolutions. In case you need a few suggestions to get you started,

❑ I promise to eat candy once a day . . . and *not* just for dessert.

❑ I resolve to try new things, like the three flavors of jelly beans I've yet to sample.

❑ I promise to be a better friend/spouse/parent/child; I will share my sweets this year.

❑ This year, I will have a brighter outlook; I will see the candy bar as half *not* eaten.

❑ I resolve to find a new job that has a better candy vending machine.

❑ I resolve to take better care of myself. I will get more sleep, exercise more, take vitamins, and eat dark chocolate daily.

❑ My mottos will be *carpé diem* and *carpé candy*!

NEW YEAR, NEW YOU . . .

It's the perfect time to motivate and pursue the complete person you've strived to become. If your life was not so exciting last year, be adventurous and try dark chocolate with bacon bits or spice it up with chocolate-covered jalapeños! If last year was sour for you, try something crazy sweet, like cherry Pixy Stix or Freshen-up or Bubblicious with its cherry syrup filling. If you never want to be that vulnerable "sucker" this year, chew gummy candies like Jujyfruits and Starbursts. If you are making a jump start to eat healthy, try Bissinger's gummy bears, infused with pomegranate or açaí berries. If you are feeling old, be a kid again and lick that giant pop. Trying to be more sophisticated? Then try dark chocolate that has 98 percent cocoa. More athletic and energized? Try Quench gum or a Charge Bar! Candy allows you to rock that new persona!

CANDY-INSPIRED CULTURE

New Year's is the perfect time to enlighten your mind and soul. Why not . . .

- **SEE A SHOW.** *The Nutcracker,* for instance, will transport you to a vibrant feast of sugarplums, spice drops, and meringues.

- **VISIT AN ART GALLERY OR MUSEUM.** Some of my favorite artists use candy as the subject, such as Warhol, Koons, Kaufman, Murakami, Britto, Max, Morris, Cotton, and Albert.

- **GO TO A NAIL SALON.** Forget the fancy shoes. Get a manicure and pedicure in gorgeous candy hues that will make your toes stand out. Companies like Essie make yummy colors like Ret Hot, Cotton Candy, Candy Apple, and Marshmallow.

- **GO TO A SPA.** There are great medicinal benefits to treatments where cocoa, sugar, and vanilla are used. Get a facial with sugar scrub. Go to Bliss and have your skin regenerated with the Vanilla & Cardamon scrub or try the Chocolate Fondue Wrap at the Hershey Spa. Or better yet, Dylan's Candy Bar Re-treat products are comforting and paraben-free.

- **GET A FREE MAKEUP APPLICATION AT THE BEAUTY COUNTER.** Visit any department store's makeup counter and investigate the huge variety of candy-colored eyeliners, lip glosses, and eye shadows. Sephora is particularly fun, as they carry an array of personal care and beauty products that you can try on, experiencing the colors, smells, and tastes of candy.

- **TAKE A COOKING CLASS.** Learn how to make desserts or candy at your local culinary institute. It's even more fun to attend with friends.

- **GO TO AN ARTS AND CRAFTS STORE.** Crayola will never fail to bring back childhood memories as you read the color labels: Cotton Candy, Magic Mint, Pink Sherbet, and even Bittersweet. Benjamin Moore offers sweet options for painting your home, from Chocolate Candy Brown and Candy Cane Red to Raspberry Truffle.

- **VISIT A CANDLE STORE.** Yankee Candle has one of the largest displays of candles. The olfactory experience is amazing, and the colors resemble candy. Stock up on pumpkin and apple pie-scented candles for fall, peppermint swirl for winter.

BRAIN CANDY
NEW YEAR'S AROUND THE WORLD

New Year's is the oldest holiday. It was first observed in ancient Babylon around 2000 BC, with the first new moon after the first day of spring. Our parties today pale in comparison: the Babylonian celebration lasted for eleven days!

Different countries celebrate the start of the new year at different times—and with unique sweet treats!

- The Chinese New Year "Yuan Tan" takes place between January 21 and February 20 (the exact date is fixed by the lunar calendar). Chinese people traditionally give others red-wrapped, strawberry-flavored "lucky candies."

- In Germany, New Year's is celebrated by gifting family and friends with good-luck marzipan pigs. New Year's Eve is called Silvester, after Saint Sylvester, a pope who lived in the fourth century. December 31 is the feast day that is celebrated in his honor.

- The Jewish New Year is called Rosh Hashana, and the date varies each year according to the Jewish calendar. To ensure a "sweet new year," it's traditional to eat honey cake and also taiglach—sweet sticky cookies made from honey and nuts.

- January 1 is known in Greece not only as New Year's but also as St. Basil's Day. St. Basil, a kind and generous man, was one of the founders of the Greek Orthodox Church. On this day, Greeks bake *vasilopita* (also known as St. Basil's cake) with a gold coin inside. The cake is served in a special order: the first slice is for St. Basil; the second is for the household; and the rest is given out to the family to enjoy, from the oldest to the youngest. Whomever finds the coin in his/her piece will have luck the entire year!

CANDY ICON
BABY NEW YEAR

Since the nineteenth century, this infant has appeared on New Year's cards, candy, and decorations, typically in a diaper with a top hat and sash declaring the year. The myth states that he's a baby at the beginning of his year, but he quickly grows into an elderly bearded man by the end of his year. At the strike of midnight on New Year's Eve, he hands over his duties to the next Baby New Year.

COOKING WITH CANDY
DIY CHAMPAGNE TRUFFLES

Champagne isn't just for New Year's. You can break out the bubbly—and combine it with candy—any time a special occasion sneaks up on you: a raise, a tax refund, your favorite '80s rock band going on a reunion tour. This celebratory sweet looks fancy and tastes amazing, yet it's super simple to make.

Combine the semisweet chocolate, butter, and cream in a small bowl set over a saucepan of simmering water.

Cook the mixture, stirring constantly, until the chocolate is melted and the mixture is smooth. Remove the bowl from the pan and stir in the Champagne until combined well. Chill about 1 hour, or until mixture is completely cool.

Beat the cooled mixture with an electric mixer on medium speed about 1 minute, or until color lightens and mixture is fluffy. Chill about 30 minutes more or until mixture holds its shape.

Using a small ice-cream scoop, form the mixture into about 25 (1-inch) balls of chocolate. Place the balls on a baking sheet lined with waxed paper. Freeze about 15 minutes, until very firm. Gently roll the balls in the cocoa, chocolate shavings, or sanding sugar until coated well. Let soften at room temperature for at least 10 minutes before serving.

Makes 25 truffles

6 ounces semisweet chocolate, coarsely chopped

¼ cup (4 tablespoons) butter, cut into small pieces

3 tablespoons heavy cream

3 tablespoons Champagne

¼ cup unsweetened cocoa powder, chocolate shavings, or colored sugar for decorating

OPPOSITE: Objects on this table are more edible than they appear. Almost everything is chocolate.

CANDY WITH A KICK!

These sweets taste like liquor or are spiked with a tiny bit of alcohol, making them grown-up fun!

- Miniature chocolate liqueur bottles.

- Margarita, Strawberry Daiquiri, Lemon Drop, and Island Punch Jelly Belly beans

- Dylan's Candy Bar Kaleidoscope Cordial Mix: After Dinner Cordial Mix (Irish Cream, Peppermint Schnapps, and Toasted Almond); Celebration Cordial Mix (Champagne, Mimosa, and Margarita); Martini Cordial Mix (Appletini, Cosmopolitan, and Melontini); Night Cap Cordial Mix (Rum, Amaretto, and Cognac); Vacation Cordial Mix (Pina Colada, Strawberry Daquiri, and Mojito).

- Hotlix Pops: Tequila-flavored with a worm, Margarita sucker with salt, Piña Colada, Strawberry 49er Lollipop, and Apple 49er Gold Lollipop.

CANDY COCKTAILS
CANDY CHAMPAGNE

Add these candy touches to your bubbly and you're guaranteed a sweet new year!

DYLAN'S CANDY BAR MIDNIGHT KISS

1 serving

1 drop Angostura Bitters

1 splash Campari

Champagne

Garnish: 2 Hershey's Kisses and gummy lips

Glassware: Champagne flute

Pour the bitters, Campari, and Champagne directly into the glass and drop in the Hershey's Kisses. Attach gummy lips to the rim of the glass and serve.

**WARNING!
NOT COOL IF YOU'RE NOT 21**

DYLAN'S CANDY BAR NEW YEAR'S BLUE MOON

1 serving

1 ounce (2 tablespoons) blueberry schnapps

Champagne

Garnish: 1 blueberry lollipop or blueberry jelly beans

Glasswear: Champagne flute

Pour the schnapps and Champagne directly into the glass and drop in the blue candy accent.

PARTING IS SUCH "SWEET" SORROW...

Candy makes people happy—except when they've finished the last bite! It's always bittersweet to reach the center of the Tootsie Roll Pop, to lose the flavor in gum, or to take that last lick of the lollipop.

Endings are always tough, and ironically even then, candy is present. Whether there's a shiva service or a wake, a large banquet of confections helps to sweeten the occasion. No matter what happens in our lifetime, from wars to recessions, health epidemics to environmental challenges, candy is here to stay! It's a timeless piece of our culture that fortunately every generation can experience. By consuming candy, cooking with candy, decorating with candy, and celebrating with candy, you will live the sweet life! Give candy to someone you care about and you are guaranteed to make the person smile instantaneously, too.

I hope this book has shown you to savor life—every delicious moment of it. There's always tomorrow to taste so much more that life has to offer! May each step you take be sweet!

SOURCES & CREDITS

The following candies are registered trademarks of the respective companies:

Adams & Brooks: Whirly Pop®. Albert & Son: Ice Cubes®. American Licorice Company: Red Vines®. Annabelle Candy Co.: Abba-Zaba®, Big Hunk®, Rocky Road®. Anthon Berg: Chocolate Cordials. Bartons Confections: Million Dollar Bar®. Cadbury: Cadbury Crème Egg®. Choward's: Violet®. Espeez: Gold Mine®. Farley's & Sathers: Chuckles®, JuJubes®. Ferrara Pan: Lemonhead®, Red Hots®. Hershey's: 5th Avenue®, Good & Plenty®, Hershey's Kisses®, York Peppermint Pattie®. Just Born: Chocolate-Covered Peeps®, Peanut Chews®, Peeps®. M&M/Mars: M&M's®, Milky Way®, Snickers®, Twix®. Marpo: Marshmallow Cones®. Nestlé: Baby Ruth®, Bit-O-Honey®, Butterfinger®, Chunky®, Oh Henry!®, Sno-Caps®. New England Confectionery Company: Candy Buttons®, Clark®, Necco Wafers®. Pez: Pez®. Tootsie Roll Industries: Charleston Chew®, Dots®, Dubble Bubble®, Sugar Babies®, Sugar Daddy®, Tootsie Roll®, Wak-O-Wax®, Nik-L-Nip® wax bottles. Wm. Wrigley Jr. Company: Big League Gum®, Life Savers®, Santa's Coal Bubble Gum®. World Confections: Aerobica®.

page 11—National Confectioners Association

page 16—Polo horse, courtesy of Polo Ralph Lauren

page 16—*Willy Wonka and the Chocolate Factory* © Wolper Pictures, Limited, and the Quaker Oats Company. Licensed by: Warner Bros. Entertainment Inc. All rights reserved.

pages 16, 18, 19—Lauren family photos, courtesy of Wireimage and Polo

page 17 (top)—Magic Kingdom® Park at the Walt Disney World® Resort © by Disney Enterprises

page 17 (center)—Candy Land®, courtesy of Hasbro

page 17 (bottom)—*Alice in Wonderland,* © Disney Enterprises

page 18—Steve Kaufman "DCB" lollipops

page 19—Burton Morris "Popsicles"

page 19—Romero Britto "Candy Lover"

page 42 (top)—Candy mannequins created by the Costume Cultural Society for Dylan's Candy Bar

page 42 (bottom)—*Project Runway* dresses courtesy of Carson's Wrapped Hershey's Chocolate

page 60—Dylan's Candy Bar Barbie® doll by Mattel

page 61—Dylan's Candy Bar Candy Land® Game, courtesy of Hasbro

page 139—Courtesy of Radio Flyer Company

page 140—Candy Land Game Bucket, courtesy of Macbeth Design, Inc.

pages 150–151—Courtesy of Jelly Belly Candy Company, by Peter Rocha

page 158—Michael Albert, "Etude-Candy Logos A to Z," 2002

page 213—Malcolm West, "Statue of Harry Gordon Selfridge," courtesy of Selfridges and Jelly Belly Candy Company

INDEX

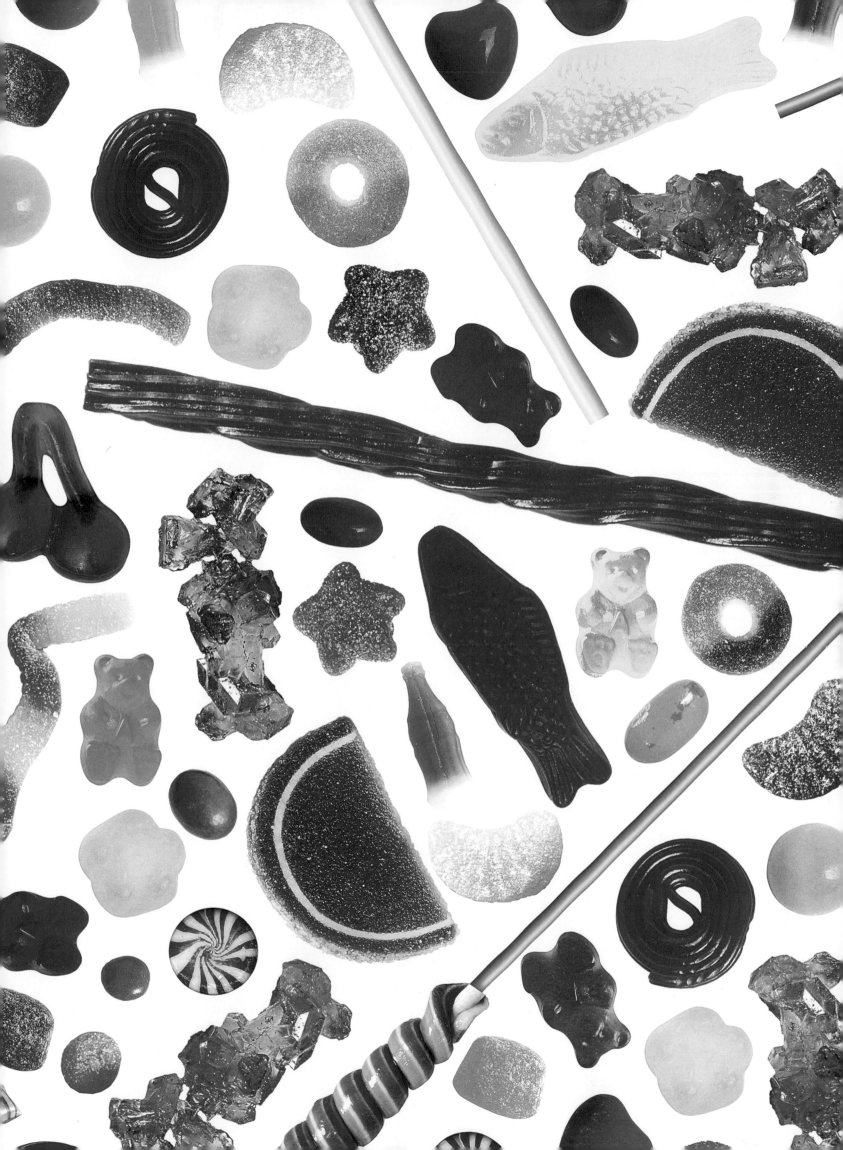